THE ENFP CALLING

DEFY THE ZOMBIE ROBOTS AND CREATE YOUR LIFE OF FREEDOM, FUN, AND FULFILLMENT

DAN JOHNSTON

EDITOR – TARA NELSON

DESIGN & ILLUSTRATIONS – MILA PARSEC

COVER DESIGN – GABU MILFORD

Legal Stuff

The ENFP Calling © 2023 by Dan Johnston. No part of this publication may be reproduced, distributed, or transmitted in any form or by any means, including photocopying, recording, or other electronic or mechanical methods, or by any information storage and retrieval system without the prior written permission of the publisher, except in the case of very brief quotations embodied in critical reviews and certain other non-commercial uses permitted by copyright law.

Written and Published by Dan Johnston.
Edited By Tara Nelson
Designed and Illustrated by Mila Parsec
Cover Designed by Gabu Milford

First Edition

Myers-Briggs Type Indicator, Myers-Briggs, and MBTI are trademarks or registered trademarks of the MBTI® Trust, Inc., in the United States and other countries.

The information in this book is intended to improve your life but it does not replace specific, professional advice in any way, nor is it legal, medical, financial, or psychiatric advice. So, if you're in a bad place or may be suffering from a mental illness, please seek professional help.

DEDICATION

This book is dedicated to ENFPs everywhere, past and present, alive and dead. Except the dictators. Well, okay, to you as well because I bet you had good intentions at the start.

I'm grateful to Andrew, Sena, Marina, Noah, and Cecelia for your contributions. Your kind words and points for improvement helped make this book what it is.

I'd like to thank everyone in my ENFP Unleashed community. Our time together, especially on the live training and group coaching sessions, is always a source of inspiration and fuel for me and a great source of new ideas—some of which made it into this book.

I'm appreciate everyone who has followed my YouTube, Podcast, or Instagram, or who reads all my emails...or at least some of them. Without you I'd just be another crazy person shouting my ideas into the dark.

I'd also like to thank Tara, an INFP and my editor on this one, for sticking with me through the total re-write. Thank you for your insights, input, and, well, not killing me.

I'm forever grateful to Mila for having my back and saving my ass on this book.

Last, I'd like to thank my Mom (ESFJ) and Dad (ENTJ). While I'll never know if your structured parenting saved me from a life as a creepy broke hippy, or held me back from a career in comedy, I'll always be grateful for having two parents who loved me, cared about me, and believed in me in absolute abundance. I would never have felt so free to fly from the nest if I didn't know I had such a strong nest to return to if things went astray.

Table of Contents

FOREWORD

I'm going to just rewrite the whole book. There is too much compromise. Too much fluff.

My editor was not particularly excited by this.

People don't come to me for play it safe advice. They have plenty of people in their lives telling them how to compromise, how to settle, how to play it safe. They come to me because they know I can be that one voice, that one person in their life telling them "There is more. You're possible of much more than you know. You don't need to compromise. You don't need to play it safe."

What a disservice I would do them if I chose to play it safe and write this book "to the middle." How could I live with myself if I published something that could be used as an excuse for someone to settle for less than they deserve?

"So, you really want to re-write the whole book? You know it is supposed to be published in 13 days."

Want to, absolutely not. I need to. There is no other way.

And Here We Are

It turns out I didn't hit my 13-day deadline. In fact, in the end, I scrapped 95% of what I had previously written and wrote a new book from the ground up. Then I shared it with some of my former clients for their input and made a series of revisions and additions.

If you like to travel, perhaps you'll find some joy in knowing parts of this book were written in: Serbia, Romania, Montenegro, Germany, Spain, and Czechia.

I know, I know, everyone wants "made local" these days... I guess I've just never been very good at following trends.

INTRODUCTION

You've probably seen that other book for ENFPs out there: The Survival Guide. It is, well, a guide for surviving. You know, moving from struggling to some kind of acceptable average where you can get by and get along in your surroundings.

This book is entirely different. I believe ENFPs have been given an incredible set of abilities and are obligated to use those abilities for the greater good.

Perhaps it is a radical idea, but hear me out. Imagine it's back in the day and you're living in a village of 100 people. 99 of the 100 have no musical ability whatsoever. One of the villagers, one of the 100—let's call her Jules—just so happens to be an incredible singer.

> If Jules chooses to, she will bring joy, dance, and transformation to those in her village. If she doesn't, not only will she miss out on her favorite thing to do, singing, but the villagers will not get to dance. Her community will miss out on one of life's great joys and be worse off because of it: Worse hunters, worse fishers, worse berry pickers, worse partners, parents and grandparents, leaders and shamans.

All these people will be worse off because one person, blessed with the gift of song, chose not to sing.

Call me crazy, but if you ask me, Jules is an asshole if she doesn't sing. I don't care if Jules's parents said it would be safer to become a coconut counter. I don't care if Jules's uncle once made a joke about her voice. I don't care if Jules gets a little nervous before she has to perform. None of her reasons for staying silent matter: If Jules doesn't sing, her people can't dance. Jules owes it to those she loves and her wider community—the world at large—to use her gifts to bring joy.

My fellow ENFP, the people are begging to dance. From the street corners of LA to the rooftops of Tokyo, from the beaches of Brazil to the cafes of Paris...

It is our time. *Together* we can make them dance.

We must. Because it is our calling. We have been given the gift of inspiration and the ability to move people to a better life. Whether you're a contractor empowering your workers to have a better life, an artist inspiring others with your creativity, or a teacher or parent inspiring the young ones...by living your calling you will empower dozens, if not hundreds or thousands of others to see new possibilities, believe in themselves, and ultimately play the game of life at a higher level.

WARNING

If the book cover and introduction weren't enough, here is your final warning: This book contains no compromises. No safe bets. No middle ground.

If you're currently settling in one or more areas of your life (and we all are), be prepared to experience some pretty significant resistance. Be ready for that voice to pop up telling you this Dan guy is an idiot, a loony, a dreamer, doesn't know what he's talking about. He doesn't know you and your struggles.

Be prepared to question everything about your life and seriously consider big, uncomfortable changes.

It was not comfortable when I moved to Costa Rica with less than a month's living expenses in the bank to start my location independent life (now going on 11 years). Who knew the enthusiasm and motivation that came from following my dreams would propel me to triple my income within a few months of reaching my mango paradise?

It was not comfortable. In fact, it was downright uncomfortable and embarrassing when I carried a sack of coins, my last €40, into a phone store in Italy to purchase a calling card so I could stay afloat while trying to make my coaching business work. A smarter person would have called it quits and moved back to Canada months before.

It certainly was not comfortable or pleasant when I realized I needed to end my 6 year relationship. During all these years, the thought had never crossed my mind. I had been all in.

It was a painful few months as I mulled over the decision, spoke to friends and professionals, and considered perhaps the biggest change I'd ever make (and this is from a guy who has lived in 10 countries!). Deep down I knew it was right. I knew I was going down a path that was taking me away from my own calling, my purpose. A path that would lessen my ability to be my true self, to have an impact on the world, and ultimately lead to unhappiness.

It was an extremely difficult decision to make and a painful conversation to have but it was the right one for me and one I haven't regretted.

I will understand if you aren't ready to make any changes, if now is a time of comfort for you, and you decide to put this book down. I will understand if you do, but I hope you won't. I hope you'll stick with me.

Some People Make Life Way Too Difficult

"You are what you settle for."—Janis Joplin

I've done my best to filter people from the outside. Heck, the cover of this book screams "if you don't want to go all in, buy another book!"

Still, those with "bad luck" or who live in survival mode tend not to notice these things.

One of my favorite studies asked participants to describe themselves as "lucky" or "unlucky". Dr. Wiseman then timed how long it took participants to count the amount of pictures in a newspaper. Researchers were blown away: The lucky group was exponentially faster! How was this even possible?

Well, because there was a half-page ad with massive type that said "Stop counting. There are 42 photographs in this newspaper." Another ad said "Tell the experimenter you've seen this ad and collect your $100 now."

Yes, the self-described unlucky group didn't notice this while the lucky group did. Could it be possible that these "unlucky" people miss other opportunities and gifts waiting for them in clear sight? Yes, like in those cheesy romantic comedies when the two people waste 2 hours of our time before figuring out they were perfect for each other the whole time.

IT IS RIGHT THERE IN FRONT OF YOU!

I fully expect that as some people read this book, there will be a voice in their head that, if it hasn't already, jumps in with "this guy doesn't know what he's talking about. Life isn't that simple. He doesn't understand that x, y, and z happened to me..."

Everyone on the planet will have perfectly legitimate reasons why they shouldn't follow their heart and chase the life they want. "I have kids." "I have a medical condition." "I have a ton of student debt." "I *can* do it, and I *want* to, but now is just not the best time..."

I must confess, even as I write some of these sections, a voice in my head pops in, coming to your defense. "Dan, come on, maybe their life isn't so simple..."

I've decided that the world would be better if, like most sports commentators, that voice just shut up. Who am I to limit what you're capable of? Who am I to limit your choices and possibilities before you've even tried? Who am I to condemn you to a life of lower standards?

No matter how real they are, your reasons can only hold you back if you choose to believe them.

I know it's hard sometimes, believe me. Aren't I the guy who had a painful public business failure and still refused to take a job or quit on the dream after? The guy who would choose between buying pasta sauce or a coffee at Starbucks so that I could use it as an office for the day?

Aren't I the guy who was down to my last $40 while living in Italy, with rent coming due, and who spent it on a long-distance plan so I could close a $10,000 contract and keep my dream alive?

Right. I am that guy.

So why should I expect anything less from you?

Life isn't always simple and it certainly isn't always easy. But what's the alternative?

If your family and longtime friends are anything like mine used to be, then I know you have no shortage of people giving you safe and rational advice. What value would I be if I echoed that?

Instead, I'm going to lay out an alternative attitude, mind-set, and approach that's at least as valid as playing it safe. Perhaps far more valid.

My point is not that you need to abandon your kids or start skipping debt payments, but instead, that these aren't *really* the things that will prevent you from living your dreams. You're still in control of your life and you can still make significant leaps in the direction you want to go.

What you decide to do is always *your* choice. Now, at least, you'll have another perspective to think about.

My long-time client, friend, and editor shared this metaphor to capture my approach as a coach, and my message in this book:

> Metaphorically, this book isn't saying I know your dream is to fly but "Don't jump off that cliff because you don't have wings. You can't fly." Nor is it saying, "jump off the cliff! If you put your mind to it, you'll fly."

> It's saying: "If your dream is to soar, let's not let your lack of wings stop you. let's find you a pilot's license, a glider, or a jetpack. Heck, let's build a freakin' zipline if we need to but don't you dare keep your feet firmly planted in the dirt."

If you wait for the right moment, you might be waiting a while. What if you already have everything you need? What if you're already ready? What if you wouldn't know you were ready even if you were? Wouldn't it be best to stop waiting around then?

You're an ENFP. We both know we'd rather have a challenging life with Hollywood-inspired moments of failure and triumph than ride the boring express straight to retirement.

There's more to life than a stable job and a retirement package. My advice to you is and always will be this: Choose your dream, buckle your seatbelt, and take a ride. A Lamborghini deserves more than just a garage.

Christina Was Not Making Excuses

"Oh wonderful". I will admit, my first thoughts upon meeting Christina were not the most positive. Her initial vibe screamed American helicopter parent as she dictated very specific breakfasts each of her 4 kids would be having to the hotel chef. She seemed more than a little out of place in Rwanda.

I decided to avoid the circus and take my breakfast to my room.

Later that day I regretted being so judgmental, although I still appreciated having my breakfast in peace.

"We're moving here," Christina told me. "We're touring the country now and trying to find the right town to live in."

WHAT?!

If you've never been to Rwanda you need to know a few things:

1. There are no tourist towns or resorts.

2. Nearly every white person there is a tourist who came to see Gorillas, an NGO worker, or a missionary.

I didn't see any crosses nor did I spot a husband dressed for an NGO job.

Christina shared they were coming from Albania. "We spent a few years there. It's such a beautiful country and the people are so kind." Before that was Vietnam and somewhere in Central America—I forget (I was a little overwhelmed at this point!).

Her kids seemed to be responsible, got along well together, and from my count, spoke some Spanish, Vietnamese, and even a bit of Albanian. Now they would be living in Rwanda for at least a year. Perhaps, just maybe, is it possible that instead of children being a reason to not pursue dreams, they can be one of the best reasons to do so? Does anyone think Bobby seeing his parents slave away at the office for "his security" is really the ideal outcome.

SO, YOU'RE AN ENFP... CONGRATULATIONS

Whatever you think you know about being an ENFP is about to be turned upside down. Now, let me clear the dance floor because you're about to bust a celebratory move.

THE ENFP NEEDS MOTION

I hate packing but I can't seem to stop moving.

My host chuckled.

It was the third time I was packing up my possessions in the same number of months. During my first five weeks in Belgrade, Serbia, I lived in a four-star hotel, then a tiny studio, and I'm now concluding a fortnight in a humongous designer flat shared with my mom and a former client turned friend, Tara.

I know you're neither my real estate agent nor my therapist. I share these details because it paints a picture of a few key ENFP traits:

We follow our hearts and are willing to shake things up in the process.

We're flexible and find different things to enjoy about different experiences.

We're always moving.

These characteristics are as natural to us as our DNA. They can lead to positive effects and perhaps a few negative ones (let's call them "learning experiences") from time to time, but it's pretty much impossible for us to stop doing them.

For me, my constant movement is both figurative and literal. Belgrade was the fourth city I lived in in two years—during a pandemic. I started off in Spain, spent the summer in Germany, winter in the Algarve in Portugal, and then moved here.

Part of the movement was for visa purposes, some to outrun new virus waves, and some for the weather. But more importantly, I moved because I wanted to. If I'm going to be locked inside for months at a time, I'd rather stay in a Portuguese villa in the countryside than an apartment in Hamburg, Germany. I know I have the freedom to choose and I don't like settling.

Neither do most ENFPs, but we focus on different things than most people. We can be fine with staying in a crappy studio apartment if we need to: We've got nothing to prove. As long as the bed is comfy enough, I'm good.

But what ENFP turns down the opportunity to improve themselves, their life, and their lifestyle?

That's the real reason I've been moving since 2012. What started as a quest to find my perfect spot became the realization that my life is better when I can "winter" somewhere sunny. Why settle for one home when I could have two or three?

I've come to realize that there will never be a "perfect spot" for me, because the contrast and motion between places is what keeps my life exciting. There's no end goal that I'm trying to work toward, where once I achieve it, I'll be done and sit on my ass for the rest of my life. *Enjoying and engaging with the process is the goal.*

Ever since I realized that, I've felt a lot less guilty for following my heart and changing what I want to change.

How ENFPs Move

Our movement isn't always by plane, train, or automobile.

It's also our minds that never stop. My ex-girlfriend, an ENFJ, said I moved everything: shoes, headphones, suitcases—heck, I was in this latest hotel for just six days before I rearranged the furniture into an *obviously* superior setup.

ENFPs move things. We move relationships: sometimes forward, and sometimes from one to another a little too quickly. We move companies: sometimes forward, and sometimes from one to another a little too quickly. We move sentences: sometimes forward, and sometimes...

We move people. We move groups—to tears, to joy, to shouts, and to laughter. We even occasionally move culture itself.

We move when we see, or at least suspect, there is a better way of doing things or simply being. Sometimes we're right and our movement immensely improves our lives and the lives of those we love. Other times, well...you can't score every basket, right?

When you love the feeling of forward movement and feel the benefits of the growth it brings, you never want to settle or settle down.

You never stop moving, you never stop changing, and you always push things a little further.

For years, my father seemed convinced that I was moving to avoid hard work, getting serious, or growing up. He thought I was running from life.

Eventually, after visiting me in Prague and seeing the life I had there, I think he realized I'm not moving from life; I'm moving to create life, *my* life.

Owning It

Seeing as I've just told you about living in villas and hotels, traveling the world during a pandemic, and my ambition to own many homes in many countries, I can't help but pause and worry. Do I sound arrogant here? What if people don't understand why we had to travel during the pandemic? What about...

Stop it. No, you stop it!

Our curse is always worrying if people will like us and at times, shrinking our ambitions or successes to blend in and be "socially acceptable," whatever the hell that means.

Some advice for you and me both is that we should fight the urge to make ourselves smaller, limiting our dreams and holding back our successes because we're scared someone won't like us. That will be a recurring point throughout this book. I implore you to *never* compromise on your biggest dreams for your career, relationships, lifestyle, and happiness. I promise you will see some huge results very quickly if you choose to follow this advice.

Don't pretend you don't want what you want and don't stop moving until you get it.

Do it for you.

"Our deepest fear is not that we are inadequate. Our deepest fear is that we are powerful beyond measure. It is our light, not our darkness that most frightens us. We ask ourselves, who am I to be brilliant, gorgeous, talented, fabulous? Actually, who are you not to be? You are a child of God. Your playing small does not serve the world. There is nothing enlightened about shrinking so that other people won't feel insecure around you. We are all meant to shine, as children do. We were born to make manifest the glory of God that is within us. It is not just in some of us; it is in everyone. And as we let our own light shine, we unconsciously give other people permission to do the same. As we are liberated from our own fear, our presence automatically liberates others ."
—Marianne Williamson

WHAT'S THE POINT OF IT ALL?

"The only thing that is ultimately real about your journey
is the step you are taking at this moment. That is all there
ever is." —Alan Watts

One takeaway from this book is going to be that for an ENFP, perhaps more than any other type, we really must enjoy the journey.

Because we create so much change around us, we paradoxically seek out permanence. We want to find the perfect morning routine or the one career we can stick to. We love the idea of passive income, selling a business, or early retirement. We have this feeling like "If I can just get to X, everything will fall into place."

Of course, it isn't just ENFPs who have these thoughts, but as the masters of change and adventure, we're perhaps the least likely to be happy with anything permanent.

In 2021 I moved into my dream apartment in Prague. It's an incredible apartment in all ways. It's huge, right on the best part of the river, has 3 balconies, a BBQ, sauna, and gym inside the flat as well as perhaps the best view in Prague from my office. It is more than I would ever want or imagined I'd have and yet...

Shortly after moving in, I found myself visiting Paris for a month and noticed I was *just as happy* living in a bachelor apartment.

Sure, when I'm home I appreciate all the luxuries: I really, really love the sauna and the views. Yet, I think my happiness dropped after moving into the apartment.

As someone who has ticked off some big goals, such as publishing a book, starting his own business, or giving an Italian woman an orgasm, I can tell you that enjoying the journey is everything. Sure, my life has improved after each of these accomplishments but there is no magical end point. I have never reached a goal and then thought "Wow, okay, now I've finally made it."

I (and I am guessing, you) *need* variety, challenge, and adventure. This means we will always be expanding ourselves and taking on new things, so we must learn to enjoy the journey and become comfortable handing challenges, dealing with problems, and moving forward.

With that said, just because we're going to be enjoying the journey doesn't mean we shouldn't have a destination in mind.

L'amore è un viaggio non una destinazione.

Discovering Your Calling

As you read this book, you'll learn more about ENFP strengths and start to uncover your own calling. I will never prescribe a purpose or calling for you, but I may suggest criteria and give some hints along the way.

This book is written—ahem, rewritten—around one core and uncompromising idea: It is my obligation as your guide here to help you move towards self-actualization.

Where We Are Going

▸ Self-awareness, self-acceptance, and high self-confidence

▸ Spending as much of your time as possible working in your strengths and using your gifts.

▸ Surrounding yourself with people who support you becoming your highest self.

▸ Being authentic and true to yourself and loving the full range of your personality, from deep wisdom and insights to playful fun, laughter, and adventure.

Oh, and Maslow didn't specifically mention this, but last up is my desire for you to have an incredible life packed with adventures, hilarious stories, and more love than a Hugh Grant movie... but hopefully a lot classier than Hugh Grant's real life love.

I'm also going to include elements of one of my coaching methodologies called The Life Design Approach. This approach is about starting with you and the life you want and then finding the right path to use what you're working with, such as your personality and strengths, to get the life you want.

This is in contrast to the approaches of following a conventional path, "seeing what's out there," or letting others in your life push you into what they think is best for you.

I believe with the right approach, almost anything is possible. I also believe that you can enjoy the journey. That's why my YouTube catchphrase is "helping you become the best version of yourself *while* creating the most awesome life possible for you and those you love." In other words, you can start creating that awesome life while growing and transforming yourself along the way.

One could even say that taking action to change your life is one of the best ways to change yourself.

HI, I'M DAN

I wrote the first two drafts of this book without including any "About Dan" section. During my final edit I thought it might be a good idea to include something. This is the first time we're meeting. If you're a client or longtime Podcast or YouTube subscriber, hopefully you'll learn something new as well.

First things first, you need to know I'm a kindhearted goofball who loves a good laugh so if I say something with a straight face but you feel like it must be a joke, it probably is. I read extensively and am often told I'm wise beyond my years but life is too short to take yourself too seriously, hence the poop jokes. If you don't have a sense of humor this is going to be a pretty rough read for you. Authenticity and freedom for myself and others are my top values.

> "Dan's approach is honest and personal. He's an expert in understanding people and providing advice on your own path. Oh, and he is also super funny–I've laughed my ass off more than once working with him."
> —Tamar Slooves
> Designer,Netherlands

How I Ended Up Here

While I am tempted to give you the whole biopic of my life, that would require at least three more books—after all, I am an ENFP and I've been true to my own personal value of living life to be the grandpa in the old folks' home with the coolest stories. Although if I'm honest, I've since decided I'd rather die in a blaze of awesomeness or while making love than rot away in any kind of home...but that's also a discussion for another time.

I first found out I was an ENFP from a test I did in high school. At the time I had no idea what any of this meant and disliked the teacher who tested us...so naturally I ignored it all. A few years later my mom would buy me a book about using personality type to pick your job. I never read it, but found it in my closet years later and chuckled.

I suppose at that time I was like the "bad luck" group in the study I mentioned. The answer was right there in front of me from an early age, but it wasn't until my mid 20s that I realized how valuable personality psychology was—and how dangerous it was for me to be reading business books by ENTJs.

Everything sounded great. The strategies made sense. Except, you know, I couldn't execute squat because I didn't have the personality for it.

While I understood this intellectually, it still took a few more years until it really soaked into my bones and I could go all in and embrace my passion for personality after a series of struggles and one gargantuan failure. If I'm totally honest, there are still days when, if I spend too much time around TJ types, I feel pulled to do things against my grain.

My interest in personality type has never been about personality type. If you check my YouTube channel or Instagram, you'll notice I never waste time debating someone over which celebrity is which type or the nuance of functions. To me, knowledge of our ENFP personality type is simply a tool and a massive advantage in creating the life we want. My goal is for you to use whatever knowledge I can share to get results, and ultimately create the life you want.

The Life I Created

In this book I will never prescribe a lifestyle for you but I will share bits about mine, including the pros and cons of some choices I've made.

I've always loved movement and exploration. After finishing my psychology degree, I came up with a goal: To live in five countries before I turn 30. I will admit, at the time of creating this goal, I imagined by 30 I would own penthouses in at least five counties and be taking my jet between them.

Yes, I was a pretty ambitious guy at the time. The type who took photos in a suit in front of the tallest building in the city. While I occasionally cringe at some of my old goals, I am also grateful because this materialistic ambition pushed me into a self-discovery journey which opened me up to philosophy, personal development, and positive psychology.

When I was 24, I decided to quit my work as a mortgage broker and start my own business, Elated News. My belief was that the ideas and information we put in our minds were the same as the food we put into our bodies, and that the majority of content out there was junk food for the mind. At the time, there was no "brain health food" available locally for people to read.

So I recruited writers, created the first edition, and started pitching advertisers. At this point my ability to turn an idea into reality was unquestionable. On my first day selling, two out of four businesses bought an advertising package in a magazine I'd just invented!

Now that was me in full ENFP Superhero mode...but it wasn't all sunshine and butterflies.

You might be asking, if 50% of businesses said yes to advertising, why didn't I approach 20 in a day instead of four?

Because I spent the rest of my time cowering in fear on the street. The thought of rejection—rejection of me and my idea—was so painful, it took me an hour and a lot of Jay-Z to muster the courage to enter a business.

In retrospect, this was one of my first huge insights into ENFPs and the importance of living in our strengths: When I focused on my strengths, such as recruiting writers, designing the magazine, and creating the sales materials, I was an absolute superstar. I felt amazing and unstoppable. But then, when I attempted cold calling and was faced with rejection, I became absolutely useless. Well, I still closed two sales in a day, but I'm pretty sure I slept for, like, three days after that.

In a couple of months, the first issue was being distributed. I was getting emails and calls from people who wanted to be involved. People loved the idea and wanted to help. At the same time, I was struggling with all the day-to-day stuff: Managing writers and editorial, and handling design, printing, distribution, and of course, advertising.

What suffered most? Of course, the two parts that went against my ENFP wiring: Cold sales and distribution.

Why? Both involved rejection, and I was (and still am) a sensitive guy! Distribution involved asking businesses if I could place the magazine there. And sales was sales. This created a cycle: As distribution lagged, I felt guilty about selling a magazine I knew wasn't being distributed as much or as widely as it should be. This messed with my head, editorial got behind, and everything suffered.

Then I came up with a great idea! I would recruit a team of sales people in the most ENFP way possible. I announced a contest! I would train students and recent graduates in sales and whoever sold the most over a month would, in addition to their commissions, get an epic prize. I called in favors with a few friends who were professional coaches and sales trainers and we put together an awesome two-day sales training session.

This next month was awesome. A few superstars emerged and we ended up with a ton of new advertisers and a wealth of enthusiasm for Elated News.

Then...the contest ended and I just defaulted to maintenance mode. I kept the two standout salespeople on board and looked for an assistant or partner. I knew I was doing too much and I was definitely not capable of doing everything.

I made some big mistakes during the final months, many of which were related to the struggles of a young ENFP, such as getting an expensive office based on *very ambitious* projections.

In the end, the business failed and I was—excuse my French—totally fucked. I'd went all in, which included using all my credit cards to fund whatever I could. I literally sold my phone to pay my assistant the last $500 I owed her.

OK, so that sucked. And yet, I can't imagine it going any other way.

> "You were becoming a real arrogant little shit you know. I think the failure was good for you". —My Mom

My entrepreneur friend Mike used to always say "I'm not scared. If my business fails I'll just go back to bar tending. That was a really fun time in my life."

Unfortunately, in Vancouver, you only start as a bartender if God has blessed you with incredible cleavage. If you're Dan, you work as the assistant to the assistant to the bartender. This means when someone pukes in the urinal, well, it's on you.

Also unfortunately, after my business failure I owed a friend $2,000 and that friend, just my luck, happened to be managing a western bar.

So here I am—a few weeks ago, wearing suits, managing a team, trying to change lives—cleaning cowboy puke.

If you're Dan, you also have the luck that a group of guys from university you never really got along with just happen to come to the bar that night. Whether or not it was their puke, I'll never know, but it certainly wasn't an easy hit for my ego.

While I did enjoy flirting with the bartender (the one with no experience but much better cleavage than mine), cleaning cowboy vomit till 4 a.m. left me sick after just two days. On Monday I decided I needed to do something to earn money minus the bodily fluids. After 48 hours of contemplation, I decided on freelance writing with a focus on copywriting.

> The time pressure was a massive help here. I didn't have time to wait for a message from the universe in my pasta. I simply thought "well, I like writing, I've enjoyed learning about advertising for Elated News, so let's do it!"

Within a day I put up a note on Facebook announcing my new profession and I had my first two clients contact me that day. Yes, it really was that easy. I even have a screenshot of the Facebook note I shared on my blog. You can find a link to the article on this book's resource page: www.DreamsAroundTheWorld.com/Calling

I spent the next year working as a freelance writer, minus some natural shiny object distractions like creating a startup with four friends on the side. I was surviving, but just barely; I'd rented out every square inch of my apartment to drop my own rent down to $250 and was living cheap.

I'd all but given up on my living-in-five-countries-before-30 dream when a friend of mine brought it up: "You know, you could just write from the other countries."

What an idea. This was 2012, before the days of Zoom and the widespread acceptance of remote work, so there was a lot of fear about losing clients, but hey... Fuck it. What was the worst that could happen?

I looked at flights and found a good one I could get on airline points (I still had those from all the credit card debt). I drank too much wine to get over the last-minute fear, follow my 20 seconds of courage approach you'll learn about shortly, and booked my flight to Costa Rica via New York!

I was supposed to move to Costa Rica with my friend Will. We were going to share an apartment which we figured would be around $800 a month, so $400 a month each. Will decided to bail at the last minute and Costa Rica decided to be way more expensive than I assumed. So I decided to turn back and wait until I saved up some more money, right?

Of course not! I hate fees and there was no way I was going to pay a rebooking fee on my flight. I went all in, figuring I could always earn a few bucks as an exotic dancer. Hey, in Costa Rica, a 6'4 Canadian guy WOULD be very exotic!

If you know me, you know I'm not overly woo-woo, but I can only explain what happened next as the universe saying "you picked yourself up again, you went all in, you earned this" and parting the sea for me.

Within 2 months of living in Costa Rica, I was earning enough money that, in addition to affording my $1,100 month rent and taking trips around Costa Rica, I had enough extra cash to fly my brother down for a 2-week vacation with me.

Now, some of you might say "But Dan, you had just gone bankrupt, and you'd been broke for a year. Wouldn't it be wise to save up that extra money for a rainy day?"

While Dave Ramsey would totally agree with you, I've never been motivated by money. I've always been motivated by people. The idea of bringing my brother so much joy by surprising him with a flight to Costa Rica felt much more powerful than saving a few thousand for a rainy day.

Also, why is anyone surprised by my lack of financial prudence?

I literally told you that my framework for life was to be the Grandpa with the coolest stories.

After that summer in New York, I moved to Europe, where I've been ever since. I have lived in many countries, traveled to more, and spend most of my time learning, writing, creating, and coaching awesome people. I have a life of total freedom, doing what I love, surrounded by a community of authentic, interesting, and fun as hell people, and *I owe it all to falling on my ass.*

It isn't until this very moment, finally writing out my story, that I have connected the dots: If I didn't go all in and fail so spectacularly, I would never have become a writer nor would I have achieved my goal of living in five countries before I turned 30. Instead of swimming in culture and adventure, on track to being that Grandpa, I might have ended up as just another guy chasing a buck back home.

> I believe that it is only by embracing who we are and going all in that we can give ourselves the opportunity to live as we're meant to. Don't half-ass things and I promise you'll be rewarded... you might just have to clean a little puke along the way.

If you're like me, you don't much of a push to want to learn from someone. I believe I can learn something from everyone, and at the same time, I try not to believe everything anyone says without thinking it through. I also know time and attention are valuable and I think it's important to learn from people who walk the talk.

So here, I'll reluctantly share a few of my external accomplishments that might be relevant if you prefer to learn from someone who walks the walk versus taking a more academic approach:

- I've created two successful location independent businesses, first as a freelance writer and then as a coach and trainer.

- I've lived in a total of ten countries while growing two international businesses, with clients from dozens of countries.

- While dealing with a business failure and bankruptcy I grew my freelance writing business, successfully raising my hourly rate from $16 to $125 in a year.

- In my late 20s, I thought up, wrote, and published two series of books—11 books in total—in under 18 months. Altogether, I ended up selling well over 10,000 books.

- I've built a successful YouTube channel with 63,000 subscribers and hundreds of videos as well as a popular podcast.

I cringe a little, sharing accomplishments like these, but I do think it's important to establish that I have figured out how to break that ENFP curse and follow through, bringing important projects to completion.

While I'm sure there's more I could add above, it's more important to me that I did the above while living life to the fullest and creating some pretty incredible experiences and memories for myself and the people I care about.

Now to keep this book fun and authentic and prove I'm an ENFP, here are nine truths and one lie.

- I'm deathly allergic to peanuts. You need to know this to make sense of a few jokes in this book, and also in case you ever come to one of my parties. Please don't bring peanuts.

- One time while in Mexico hosting the first Life Design Fiesta event, I found myself life coaching a cartel boss in an Irish bar for hours. It was one of the most surreal experiences of my life.

- I was inspired by a Mathew McConaughey movie to become a Big Brother. We were likely their most successful match in history, staying together officially for 4 years. Later, I found out he was an INTJ and we recorded a podcast about it all. You can find it on the resources page.

- Panos is an ENFP from Cyprus who once won a travel show based on circling the world by making friends. One night we were trading travel stories. Having never been to Africa and feeling inspired, I impulsively booked a flight to Rwanda. It ended up being one of the best trips of my life.

- While living in New York, I bought an expensive suit that I couldn't fit as motivation to fit it. Also, it was awesome and 50% off. Eventually it fit.

- Despite what looks like risk taking, I never try something new unless I have at least 12 months living expenses in the bank and a plan B.

- When traveling abroad I used to get stopped in the streets and mistaken for Mathew Fox, aka Jack from Lost. I'm not sure if this stopped happening because Lost went off the air or because I got a better haircut.

- One time in Barcelona I met a real life James Bond. Turns out he was really into psychology and we had an incredible six-hour bromance geeking out over our favorite theories. Then, having no contact information, he disappeared from my life forever.

- I once spent 24 hours in Vienna with a woman I met for the first time on the train there. Yes, like that movie Watch Before Sunrise, which I still haven't seen.

- When I was very young, I was struggling in school and so my parents sent me to get tested. My parents were told I scored genius level in maths and logic but would always struggle with speaking and language.

Reader Resources

There was SO MUCH I wanted to include in this book. Some ended up in the appendix while other parts I feel are really valuable just didn't fit between these pages. So what I've done is create page of resources for you. You can find the main resource page here:
www.DreamsAroundTheWorld.com/Calling

As well, there are a few extra gems scattered through this book, such as a 7 day audio program or one hour training on entrepreneurship. These are all totally free, but you'll need to read on to find the details.

How I Support My Fellow ENFPs

Throughout this book you might hear me mention something I learned from a client or that happened at one of my events. To keep the confusion to a minimum, I'm going to share a brief nugget on each of the main ways I work with ENFPs.

- **ENFP Unleashed** is a 12-week training which includes live coaching and a supportive community. It includes extras like the Superstar Series where I interview ENFPs who have achieved incredible things and get into detail about how they did it. As of this writing, I personally host group coaching sessions with members at least a few times a month.

- **One-on-One Coaching.** My availability for one-on-one coaching varies tremendously by my writing and travel schedule, but you can always check my availability on the Work with Me page of my website.

- **In Person Events:** I try to host one multi day in person event a year if time allows and enough people are interested.

▶ **The Free Freelancer** is an intensive training program I run once per year for all NF types, although the members are mostly ENFPs. The program is for anyone who intends to build a successful freelancing, consulting, or coaching business and wants to learn business and marketing strategies specifically for NF types. I believe ENFPs want win-win relationships and care as much about giving value and having a positive impact as they do about making money and the lifestyle benefits of entrepreneurship.

For more details on all of the above and links to the specific pages, you can visit www.DreamsAroundTheWorld.com/Further

"Having the support of Dan has given me the confidence and courage to just carry on and I'm now at the position where I'm really excited about the future.
 I think that for the first time I have a clear goal, I know where I'm going and I finally feel like I'm on the right path!"
—Kelly Parker, UK

PERSONALITY PSYCHOLOGY & THE ENFP FUNCTIONS

Your type simply reflects your preferences and most natural way of operating. It does not decide who you are, who you will be, or what you're capable of.

That power, and responsibility, rests with you.

DISCOVERING THE CAMPAIGNER

The next few sections cover some important basics of the ENFP personality that will help you get the most from this book. Think of it as eating your veggies before dessert. If you're a vegetarian this is wonderful. If you're a sugar addict you may consider skipping ahead if you start to get bored and coming back to finish this section when you're ready for your veggies.

At this point, I'm going to assume you're an ENFP and are reading about yourself or reading about someone you care about who is an ENFP.

I'm also going to assume you've read some of the basic descriptions online about ENFPs and have bought this book because you want depth and details on how ENFPs can thrive.

So with that said, I won't bore you with a drawn out description of ENFPs. I'll keep it short and let you get on to the other chapters where we go deeper into specific areas like career and relationships.

ENFPs delight in movement and are often the catalyst for change on a societal level. While they are often bored with the details and may struggle to follow through on plans, ENFPs have an incredible ability to initiate change and get the ball rolling.

This stems from a combination of three ENFP abilities:

1. ENFPs are able to develop a unique, uncompromising, and inspiring vision for the future.

2. ENFPs have a dislike for the established, be it rules, ways of doing things, or authority. This inspires them (and others) if they choose to take on an established organization or way of thinking, and provides them with an almost unlimited source of energy.

3. An ENFP's enthusiasm, charisma, and inspiring vision for the future act as a natural magnet and attracts people to their cause. An ENFP on a mission will soon find themselves surrounded by dozens, if not hundreds or thousands, of people willing to put it all on the line to help the ENFP achieve their vision.

In all they do, ENFPs bring a liveliness and sense of play to life. This makes them fun co-workers, friends, and partners. When they focus on their strengths, ENFPs excel. When they move outside their strengths, ENFPs can still find a marginal level of success, but will not be as happy or perform at their best.

One challenge for the ENFP is that they can be good at many things because they are naturally intelligent, quick learners, and very adaptable. This leads many ENFPs down a path of mediocrity. ENFPs must not settle for good and instead should seek opportunities to use their true strengths and become great.

Another common scenario for ENFPs is the search for their purpose or the sweet spot where they really do excel. This is a good path for the ENFP, but can appear to be unfocused to the outside world. In the Kryptonite chapter we talk about this "Shiny Object Syndrome" and how to overcome it.

Overall, ENFPs are fun, optimistic, and caring individuals who want the best for themselves and the people around them. When they discover themselves and focus on their true purpose, an ENFP is capable of tremendous levels of success and of making a positive impact on the world.

IN GOOD COMPANY: FAMOUS ENFPS

As an ENFP, you are among some very good company. In this chapter you'll find a collection of famous and successful people who are either confirmed or suspected to be ENFPs. Note that there is always intense debate around typing celebrities and there have always been differing opinions online. I've built this list from multiple sources, giving it my best guess.

Do not use this chapter as a guide to what you must do or who you must resemble. Rather, use this chapter as a source of inspiration. It is a chance to see what's possible as an ENFP and what great things have been accomplished by those who share a similar makeup to you.

Personally, I have found great value studying famous people from my own type through autobiographies. Most of us spend the early years of our lives feeling lost and trying to figure out our purpose or how we want to end up. I've found studying those of my type who have found their purpose, and have then achieved success, gives me a shortcut to understanding my own potential and the directions my life could go.

Writers, Creators, and Thought Leaders

- Mark Twain
- Hunter S. Thompson
- Oscar Wilde
- Aldous Huxley
- Umberto Eco
- Salman Rushdie
- Julian Assange
- Ralph Nader
- Anne Frank
- Arianna Huffington
- Walt Disney
- Kurt Vonnegut
- Osho
- Naomi Klein
- Michio Kaku
- Brian Cox
- Joseph Campbell
- Jack Ma
- Alan Watts
- Jacques Derrida

Actors and Performers

- Robin Williams
- Jerry Seinfeld
- Gwen Stefani
- Kanye West
- Ellen DeGeneres
- Keira Knightley
- Katie Couric
- Orson Welles
- Cuba Gooding Jr.
- Oliver Stone
- George Carlin
- Lil Nas X
- Jim Carrey
- Donald Glover
- Yeri (Red Velvet)
- Andy Samberg
- Jackie Chan
- SZA
- Dave Chappelle
- Awkwafina
- Jack White
- Will Smith
- Sarah Michelle Gellar
- Sharon Stone
- Sandra Bullock
- Lin-Manuel Miranda
- Fujii Kaze
- Alicia Silverstone
- André 3000
- Daniel Radcliffe

Athletes

- Yao Ming
- Tom Brady
- Kevin Garnett
- Dwight Gooden
- Jerry Rice
- Drew Brees
- Israel Adesanya

Politicians

- Ralph Nader
- Che Guevara
- Fidel Castro
- Muammar Gaddafi
- Hugo Chávez
- Andrew Yang
- Ulrike Meinhof

Worth Noting: If you haven't yet read up on any of the other types, you may not notice the distinctions of the famous ENFPs. Compared with other types, there is a heavy weighting towards writing, outside the box philosophy, and performing.

In the political arena, ENFPs aren't interested in run-of-the-mill politics. ENFPs only get involved when they're trying to right an injustice or make a massive change in the way things are done.

Of course, this is a list of famous ENFPs, so it must gravitate toward the professions that can acquire fame. No matter how successful they are, it's very unlikely you'd ever see a lawyer, doctor, or entrepreneur on a list like this, as only a tiny percentage of these professions ever acquire fame.

INTRODUCTION TO MYERS-BRIGGS®

Note: If you're well versed with the MBTI and how the functions work you may want to skip the next few sections and jump to "ENFP Strengths and Superpowers".

I first officially discovered personality psychology about five years ago. I say officially because I do have some vague memories of taking a career test in high school that was likely based on the Myers-Briggs® instrument, but who really pays attention to tests at 16?

The Myers-Briggs assessment is one of many options in the world of personality profiles and testing. It is arguably the most popular, and in my opinion, it is the best place to start. I say this because the results provide insight into all aspects of our lives, whereas other tests are often only focused on career.

The Myers-Briggs instrument is based on the idea that people are quite different from one another. These differences go deeper than emotions, moods, or environment and speak to how we're actually wired to behave.

And, as it turns out, most people end up being wired 1 of 16 ways, based on 4 groups of characteristics.

This doesn't mean we can't build certain traits or change our behavior. Rather, knowing your personality type is an opportunity to learn which traits come most naturally to you and which areas you may find challenging or need to invest time in developing.

Your type provides a platform to understand yourself and create a plan for personal growth based on your unique personality strengths and weaknesses.

It is also an opportunity to understand the people around you and get to the root of many conflicts. In fact, you may find that understanding the different types and how others relate to you is the most valuable aspect of the Myers-Briggs instrument.

The 16 types and 4 Groups

Myers-Briggs assessment includes 16 different personality types that are described by a unique series of four letters.

At first, the types appear confusing, but they're really quite simple.

Each type is based on one of two modes of being or thinking for each of the four letters.

E (extrovert) or I (introvert)

N (intuitive) or S (sensing)

T (thinking) or F (feeling)

P (perceiving) or J (judging)

Now, don't pay too much attention to the words tied to each letter because they don't actually offer a great description for the characteristic.

In just a second, I'll share my explanation for each letter. But first I want to share an important point to remember: Personality analysis and profiling is a bit of an art as well as a science. In other words, since people are so diverse, the descriptions and results aren't always black and white. Some people have a strong preference for one mode or the other, but others are closer to the middle. It's natural for all of us to occasionally feel or demonstrate traits of the other types.

What The Four Letters Mean

As you know, there are four letters that make up your personality type. At first these letters can be a little confusing, especially since their descriptions aren't the most telling.

Here's how I explain each letter.

For the first letter in your type, you are either an E or an I.

The E or I describes how we relate with other people and social situations.

Extraverts are drawn to people, groups, and new social situations. They are generally comfortable at parties and in large groups.

Introverts are more reserved. This is not to say that Introverts do not enjoy the company of people—they do. Introverts are just happier in smaller groups and with people they know and trust like friends or family. Keep in mind, this does not mean that Introverts are not capable of mastering social skills if they must. Rather, they will not be drawn to such situations or find the process as exciting or enjoyable as an extrovert would.

"The Deal Breaker": For some people E or I is obvious. For others, the line is blurred. This question will make your preference clear: "Does being around new people or groups add to or drain your energy? If you spent an entire day alone, would you feel "off" or bad, or would you be just fine?" If you can spend a day or two alone without feeling bad or if spending a few hours in a group of people leaves you feeling tired, well, then you're an Introvert.

While extraverts may often steal a lot of the attention in a room, introverts often have the upper hand. Many extraverts crave the spotlight, but introverts are able to sit back and calmly observe, learning more about a situation and making their contributions more meaningful and impactful.

On the other hand, extraverts have many advantages when it comes to first impressions, wide social circles, and the ability to have fun in large groups and make new friends.

ENFPs are extraverts. This is why ENFPs can get so much joy (and energy) from other people.

For the second letter, you are either an N or an S.
This trait describes how you interact with the world.

Those with the intuitive trait (N) tend to be introspective and imaginative. They enjoy theoretical discussions and "big picture" ideas. For an extreme example, imagine a philosophy professor with a stained suit jacket and a terribly messy office.

Of course, this isn't the reality for most N's. Most intuitive people live a happy, fulfilled life full of new ideas and inspiration... all while managing the day-to-day aspects of their lives at an acceptable level. N's have an exceptional imagination and ability to form new ideas, tell stories, and inspire those around them.

Those with the sensor trait (S) are observant and in touch with their immediate environment. They prefer practical hands-on information to theory. They prefer facts over ideas. For an extreme example, think of a mechanic or military strategist.

ENFPs have the intuitive (N) trait. This is why they are creative, great problem solvers, and drawn to big ideas.

Third, you are either a T or an F.

This trait describes how you make decisions and come to conclusions, as well as what role emotions play in your personality and how you deal with them.

Those with the thinker trait (T) are "tough-minded." They tend to be objective and impersonal with others. This can make them appear uncaring, but they are generally very fair. Thinkers rely on logic and rational arguments for their decisions. The T trait would be common among (successful) investors and those who need to make impersonal and objective decisions in their careers.

Those with the feeler trait (F) are personal, friendly, and sympathetic to others. Their decisions are often influenced by their emotions or the "people" part of a situation. They are also more sensitive, more empathetic, and more affected by their emotions. The "F" trait would be common among counselors and psychologists.

ENFPs have the feeler (F) trait.

Lastly, you are either a P or a J.

This trait describes how you organize information in your internal and external worlds. This translates into how you evaluate and organize ideas and options, assess what is possible, and maintain a schedule.

I've never liked the term "Perceiver." It is better to describe this type as "Probers" or "Explorers." These people look for options, opportunities, and alternatives. They tend to be creative and open-minded. They're also likely to have a really messy bedroom or office. Perceivers are happy to try out a plan before they have all the details because they know they can always make adjustments later on if they have to.

Judgers are structured and organized. They tend to be more consistent and scheduled. Spreadsheets may be their friends and their rooms will be clean... or at least organized. They prefer concrete plans and closure over openness and possibilities.

You would find more P's among artists and creative groups, whereas professions like accountants and engineers would be dominated by J's.

ENFPs have the perceiving (P) trait. This is one reason they are not always organized, focused, or disciplined. This is also one of the reasons ENFPs are so open to new ideas and able to come up with fresh perspectives.

The Four Groups

Since the original creation of the 16 personality types, psychologists have recognized four distinct groups, each containing four types. The four types within each group have distinct traits in common based on sharing two of the four traits.

The 4 groups are:

1. The Artisans (The SPs)

2. The Guardians (The SJs)

3. The Idealists (The NFs)

4. The Rationals (The NTs)

As an ENFP, you are an Idealist.

Idealists are abstract and compassionate. Seeking meaning and significance, they are concerned with personal growth and finding their own unique identity. Their greatest strength is diplomacy. They excel at clarifying, individualizing, unifying, and inspiring.

The other three Idealist types are:
- The Leaders: ENFJs
- The Protectors: INFJs
- The Princes and Princesses: INFPs

The ENFP's Four Functions

"I want to show the world that it is possible. It's possible to remember your self. To open your mind. To open your heart. To open your creativity. To live with less, but to live well."

—Alejandro Jodorowsky

It is important for you to know what the ENFP's four functions are, even if you don't know the science behind them. For starters, all types have the same four functions: intuition, sensing, thinking, and feeling. The differences are in how the individual uses the function (introverted vs extraverted), and the order in which the functions serve as strengths.

This will all make more sense as you read this book and continue your studies.

If it helps to get you started, here is my best attempt to explain the four functions in human terms. Many online resources use confusing technical language and psych speak when explaining this. I'll try to do the opposite here.

Think of the four functions as your four potential superpowers.

Like an RPG videogame, your starting character has certain potential abilities you can gain access to as you grow. If you select the Elf, you will have access to different powers than the Orc or the Knight.

The eight functions are:

- Extraverted Intuition (Ne)

- Introverted Intuition (Ni)

- Extraverted Sensing (Se)

- Introverted Sensing (Si)

- Extraverted Feeling (Fe)

- Introverted Feeling (Fi)

- Extraverted Thinking (Te)

- Introverted Thinking (Ti)

Note that the E or I attached to each function is not an indicator of the individual's preference for introversion or extroversion. Rather, it is an indicator of how they use the particular function.

Which four functions a type has, and their corresponding personality type, is determined by the type's preferences on the Extroversion vs Introversion and Perceiving vs Judging measures. I'm going to leave it there, as any explanation beyond this would give us both a psychology jargon headache.

In your early years, your personality is ruled by your dominant function. This shapes your early strengths as well as weaknesses. Over time, through challenges and experience, you develop your second (auxiliary) and third (tertiary) functions. You create a more powerful and balanced personality. You minimize weak spots, mature emotionally, and develop a diverse set of skills.

The key to overcoming most personality challenges is developing (strengthening) the weaker functions.

In general, we grow our primary (or dominant) function in our early years, our secondary function in our twenties and thirties, and our third function some time in our thirties and into our forties; our forties is also when we should start to make friends with our fourth function, introverted sensing.

However, this pattern assumes you're not being proactive or reading a book like this one. In your case, there is no reason you can't leap ahead a few decades and strengthen your other functions ahead of schedule. Actually, doing so is essential to your personal development.

How We Use Our Functions

In the following section, you will notice each function is described as either introverted or Extraverted. This is an indicator of use.

For example, an INFJ has "introverted intuition." This means they use their intuition to internally process ideas and situations and come to conclusions. Their secondary function is "Extraverted Feeling." This means they interact with the outside world using their feeling function. It also means most inputs are filed through the INFJ's feeling function before reaching their intuition.

An ENFP has "Extraverted Intuition" as their dominant function. This means the ENFP interacts with and experiences the outside world using their intuition. For an ENFP, their secondary function is "Introverted Feeling." This means the ENFP processes their thoughts and judgments internally based on their feelings.

An ENFP has the following functions:

Dominant Function—Extraverted Intuition (Ne): This is how the ENFP interacts and understands the outside world. Ne is about hidden meaning, alternatives, and possibilities. This function powers the ENFP's ability to create new ideas and a unique vision for the future. Their vision can then become a catalyst for action.

Auxiliary Function—Introverted Feeling (Fi): This is the ENFP's second strongest function and is used to interpret and judge the outside world against an internal set of values built around harmony and authenticity. This function gives the ENFP an ability to read between the lines and sense what is false or inauthentic in a situation.

Tertiary Function—Extraverted Thinking (Te): This is the ENFP's third function. Te strives to be efficient and productive through organization and scheduling. Te is all about logic, seeking the root cause for an action, and spotting faulty reasoning.

It should come as no surprise that developing their thinking function will help the ENFP become more organized and disciplined. It will also support them in handling confrontational situations. Exactly how to do this is addressed more in the Overcoming Your Weaknesses section, as well as in other areas of this book.

Inferior Function—Introverted Sensing (Si): This is the least developed of the ENFP's functions. ENFPs are future oriented, rarely looking over their shoulder at either the successes or disasters left in their wake. Se provides them often needed connection to the past.

Connecting With the Past

As an ENFP myself, I'm all too familiar with the fast pace and occasional chaos that can accompany our lives. Yes, this is where ENFPs thrive. We love change and challenge and have no problem with uncertainty or risk. Yet, this state of being can wear on us.

One way for us ENFPs to develop our Si (our fourth function) is to take half an hour or so a few times a month to live in the past. Not only does this develop our Si, it also provides a calming feeling and a temporary escape from the present.

Now, the key here is to complete an activity that you've done many times, providing an easy connection to the past. You should not be challenged here! Some ways to do this include building something with, for example, a Lego set or doing a puzzle you've done many times before, creating a sculpture or doing painting, listening to a familiar CD or watching a favorite show.

Ideally, the best activities involve some kind of physical activity as well, such as the building ones. With that said, one of my favorites is to rewatch the "Vegas Baby Vegas" episode of Entourage. I must have watched it 50 times now.

PART III

WHEN ENFPS ARE AWESOME

When you do what you're meant to do, and be who you're meant to be, you will be an unstoppable force for good.

ENFP STRENGTHS AND SUPERPOWERS

"To know yourself is the beginning of wisdom."
—Socrates

Strength: A trait that comes naturally that is usually positive.

Superpower: A valuable ability developed from a natural strength.

Have you ever had that experience when you're speaking with a police officer or a customs official where you feel guilty despite doing nothing wrong?

Or when the alarm beeps when you're exiting a store. You're quite sure you didn't steal anything and yet you feel bad for a moment?

If you've ever experienced this, you're not alone: Nearly everyone has. Perhaps due to similar underlying causes, many of us ENFPs do not value our strengths and instead feel guilt for not doing things how our families, friends, or colleagues would prefer us to.

ENFPs tend to develop our self-awareness earlier in life because we're curious, thoughtful, and, yes, weird. One reason ENTJs and ESTJs are disinterested in self-awareness is because they tend to fit in well with the expectations of most cultures. ENTJ men tend to be confident, competitive, ambitious and sociable. They often do well in sports, maintain their health and routines, and succeed financially. This doesn't leave a lot of opportunities for sitting back and thinking "What the heck am I doing wrong?"

Perhaps you've been surrounded by people who tell you what you can improve and how to do better rather than emphasizing your strengths. Perhaps you take your strengths for granted, so much so you're blind to your gifts.

It's time we correct this.

I'm going to start with a summary of what you might find if you were to Google ENFP strengths in case you're totally new to this or want a quick ego boost. These are important to know but aren't conclusive. The difference between a strength and a superpower is the difference between a tall Walmart clerk and an NBA star, a content writer and a beloved author, an Uber driver and an F1 racer. We're going to go deep into how you develop your strengths into superpowers that will serve you for your lifetime.

Time to discover the unique strengths closely linked to ENFPs. While you read this, remember that these are the strengths that come naturally to you, but you still need to develop and fine-tune them into superpowers if you want to thrive.

ENFPs'strengths tend to revolve around their ability to quickly absorb and process information, spot patterns, connect with people, be themselves (authenticity), and communicate in an effective and inspiring way.

Strengths come naturally to ENFPs but are not necessarily valuable until developed and focused into a superpower.

ENFP Natural Strengths

- ENFPs are "quick." They're able to quickly assess information or situations and come to surprisingly accurate conclusions before anyone else in the room does.

- ENFPs' quickness is tied to their perceptiveness and intelligence. As part of these same abilities, they're able to see connections between people, situations, and ideas that most others miss. This often leads them to create new ideas.

- ENFPs are able to quickly connect with other people and develop rapport, making those around them feel comfortable.

- ► ENFPs can quickly read a room or social situation and adapt so they fit in. They are quick on their feet and can answer a question or rebut with a joke without hesitation.

- ► ENFPs are enthusiastic, happy, and optimistic. This is often why the type is called the "Inspirer."

- ► ENFPs are extremely accepting of other people and their differences. They see people as equal and tend to believe in everyone's potential.

- ► ENFPs are generally very creative and intelligent.

- ► ENFPs are able to take in lots of information, process the important parts, and reach a decision in a quick timeframe.

- ► ENFPs are very adaptive and can function well in most situations. They're very comfortable with change.

- ► ENFPs have exceptional communication skills, both spoken and written. They're able to understand what someone is trying to say when others in the room are clueless. Similarly, they're able to communicate in a way that others can understand, almost customizing their speech to match the expectations of their audience.

- ► When connected with an issue or individual, an ENFP can become a very passionate advocate. This passion gives them the ability to inspire large groups of people or create movements.

In summary, a developed ENFP can be:

- Intelligent
- Quick
- Adaptable
- Creative
- Well-liked
- Social
- Caring
- Intuitive
- Authentic
- Supportive
- Inspiring
- Innovative

The ENFP Superpowers

Throughout this book I'm going to share with you ENFP Superpowers as well as strategies and tips to develop and use them starting with 3 superpowers to lead us off. The rest will be shared throughout the book in the sections most relevant. For example, you'll learn how ENFPs can be powerful activators in the career section.

I named each superpower after a unique role that ENFPs can play using the corresponding superpower. We tend to play these roles more when we're at our best, but when we're at our worst, we'll sometimes forget we have them at all or do the opposite. For example, the typically optimistic ENFP can become one of the most toxic Debbie Downers when things go wrong.

None of these superpowers exist in a vacuum and they play off each other quite a bit so you're sure to see connections regarding how they work together and build upon one another.

The first three superpowers all fit under one umbrella: Futuremaking. ENFPs possess an incredible ability to envision and then create a new future.

When ENFPs play futuremaking roles, we take an active role in brainstorming and creating better futures for ourselves and those we love. Keep in mind, we'll usually combine these with our people-connecting skills to get others involved to help implement our visions.

A vision turned into reality is the only vision with value, and ENFPs possess a few more abilities that allow us to make our dreams come to life.

ENFP SUPERPOWER

THE OBSERVER & LEARNER

Ironically this is going to take me longer to write because I am doing so at a cafe window in Madrid and keep being distracted by the people walking by. How I love to people watch.

I'm not alone. ENFPs have the ability to be excellent observers. We can read a room faster than anyone. We can unconsciously pick up body language and understand which couple is fighting, who is nervous, who might be into us.

Hint: According to one informal study, it might be everyone. But more on ENFPs and attraction in the relationship section.

ENFPs love to learn. Our primary function, Extraverted Intuition (Ne) feeds off novelty including new experiences and knowledge. Our interests can be incredibly diverse, both as individuals and between EN-FPs, but there's one thing you can be sure of: if someone is an ENFP they love to learn and have taken in a wealth of knowledge for their age.

When properly harnessed, the ENFP Observer understands the world around him or her more than most people and is able to draw on this wide range of knowledge and insights to discover new opportunities.

Remember, these superpowers are not guaranteed. Like all super-heroes, you must work to harness and develop your powers. I wouldn't expect an ENFP glued to Instagram to have any profound insights or opinions, nor would I expect them to notice much about the world around them. If you want to develop this superpower you must learn to be present.

And yes, I am often the one person on the tram or metro without a phone, just watching people.

Potential Superpower: The ability to develop a wide range of knowledge and insights into human nature and society.

Blocks: Distractions and not being present.

Keys to Developing:

- Put your phone away and be present in social situations.

- Put yourself into a variety of social situations. If possible, travel as much as possible.

- Ditch entertainment for education. Read or listen to classic books of both fiction and nonfiction.

ENFP SUPERPOWER

THE DREAMER

When someone takes in an abundance of information through observing and learning, there are a few possible outcomes. One is becoming a critic—someone who finds faults and flaws and points out everything people are doing wrong, highlighting the inevitable doom and gloom of the future.

Then there are those who show us the light. Those who dream of new possibilities, of a brighter future.

In the wrong state of mind, with the wrong inputs, ENFPs certainly possess the ability to be the first but fortunately for you and I, it is not our default setting. Our default setting is to be a dreamer and to inspire those around us with new possibilities for the future.

The ENFP Dreamer looks for new possibilities to make things better all around them, from suggesting how the local coffee shop could increase their sales to pointing out a talent someone never knew they had. When people say times are tough or there's no better way, the ENFP Dreamer points them to a better possibility, a better future.

Potential Superpower: To be a ray of hope and an inspirational source of new possibilities.

Blocks: Negative input. News, identity politics, and conspiracy theories will all block this superpower.

Keys To Developing:

- Proactively choose your input, including the people you spend time with and what kind of information you consume.

- Do not attempt to convert the "Debbie Downers" who only see doom and gloom...they'll pull you under with them.

- Take a moment every day to focus on what you're grateful for and what is good in the world.

ENFP SUPERPOWER

THE VISIONARY

It just so happens some of us ENFPs love to talk. One could imagine that this love of talking leads us to develop a decent ability to communicate.

We're also pretty good at seeing the big picture and connections between a diverse range of things. Thank you Ne. We're also, or so I'm told, pretty charming and can be magnetic in our energy. Now put all this together and you have our next potential superpower: The ENFP Visionary.

The ENFP Visionary first combines their observations of how things are with their optimism and belief in a better future. They then sprinkle on a healthy mix of charm and communication abilities and vola! You have an inspiring vision that people are drawn to.

Yes, in theory this could be used to start cults and spread communism... and yes... ENFPs have been guilty of both.

So I need to ask any of you with Marxist tendencies to put this book down immediately. I would offer you a refund but that would just be indulging the capitalist machine.

OK, now that we've gotten rid of the Marxists, we can continue.

This superpower is one of our most powerful and is the key to succeeding in all areas of our lives.

ENFP entrepreneurs can create a vision that attracts investors, partners, and employees. ENFP partners and parents can inspire their family to live better. This superpower is a core part of an ENFP's calling. It is with this superpower that you are able to create an exponential impact on the world without worrying about your weaknesses... because you're able to bring together a diverse group of people to work together towards a shared vision.

And yes, that means someone else can do the damn paperwork for you!

Potential Superpower: To create a magnetic vision for a better future in many areas of life.

Blocks: Poor communication or failure to think through (or articulate) some of the details.

Keys To Developing:

► Develop your communication abilities. Read a lot. Learn how to speak and present.

► Develop your ability to include some details and specifics with your big picture thinking using your Extraverted Thinking (Te).

► Don't immediately share every new idea or vision. Think it through and add a little polish before presenting it.

Keep Your Eye On The Prize

ENFPs can come up with a million solutions to any given problem, a million paths to any destination.

Use this.

Decide on an outcome. Commit to it. Write it down. Perhaps get a neck tattoo as a reminder.

Then use your creative and visionary powers to come up with different ways to get there. If one approach doesn't work, change your approach and try something else. Adjust your methods, not your outcome. If one road is blocked, find another. Buy a truck and go off road. Make friends with someone who owns a helicopter. As long as there is any hope in hell, you as an ENFP will be able to find a way if you stay focused on the outcome and keep trying new approaches.

FEEDING THE BEAST

" I was always different. Why didn't anybody notice me?
A couple of teachers would notice me, encourage me to be
something or other, to draw or to paint—express myself.
But most of the time they were trying to beat me into be-
ing a fuckin' dentist or a teacher."
—John Lennon

ENFPs thrive on new experiences that feed our Extraverted Intuition and ENFPs will do well to design their life around the ability to keep their Ne satisfied.

It's 2 p.m. and I'm sitting down at my third cafe of my writing day. Okay, the first was a cafe, the second was a Mexican restaurant, and now I'm at a beach bar.

I suppose I made the right call when, at 23, I turned down a supposedly desirable office job for the unknown. I didn't know what I wanted to do—only that I didn't want to do it locked in an office eight hours a day.

I'm not an ENTJ.

ENTJs, for those of you not overly familiar with all the types, are the classic "business executives." They're not necessarily boring; my college roommate was an ENTJ and he was always getting into trouble and having adventures. They aren't paper pushers either. ENTJs don't necessarily love routine and they can get anxious if things aren't moving forward.

But they do love, and I mean LOVE, control. It is right there in their function stack—the four functions that most affect their personality. The ENTJ's primary function is Extraverted Thinking, a judging function.

This is important to understand.

Extraverted types that start either E and end with J, (such as ENTJ, ESTJ, ENFJ) lead with a judging function. They start with how something makes them feel in the case of an ESFJ or ENFJ, or how something fits into their orderly view of the world with an ENTJ or ESTJ. Is it logical? Are they in control?

The ENTJ's primarily function is Extraverted Thinking, which is all about bringing order, structure and process to the external world. This is our third function. Remember, we are extremely strong in our primary function and relatively weak in our third function. It is also somewhere we should only spend a fraction of our time—just enough to enable our primary function.

This is why ENFPs CAN create structures, plans, and organizational systems in a burst of excitement... we just tend not to follow them for very long.

Not so with the ENTJ. ENTJs are driven by Te (Extraverted Thinking). They are driven to bring order and structure to things and ultimately to never lose control. This is why the same ENTJ who thrives in a business meeting and crushes it in his sport of choice would flat out refuse to take a dance, improv, or painting class unless he knew for sure that there was no chance of embarrassing himself or looking bad.

Our primary function drive us and ultimately shape our lives. ENTJs can love to travel, play sports, and even have the odd adventure... but good luck finding one in their 30s without a maxed out retirement account.

> ENTJ Date: "No way! I'm adventurous and I can take risks! I'm on vacation right now."
> Dan: "What percentage of your registered retirement fund contributions do you make every year?"
> ENTJ Date: "100%. OK, fine, so I'm not *super* adventurous."

ENTJs lead with judgment, followed by introverted intuition, which tends to be linked to drive, ambition, and achieving goals. And since they judge everything by Te, the ENTJ looks around in most societies and sees that the best goals involve being financially successful and respected or admired in the community. So this is where they direct their energies and ultimately the life they make.

I lead with this ENTJ example because sometimes *contrast can help us understand ourselves*, and we ENFPs—we sure as heck aren't wired one bit like ENTJs.

Our primary function is Extraverted Intuition, which is a perceiving function (we share this with ENTPs). Think of your primary function as the biggest part of your engine. If you're a titanic-sized steamship with 12 engines, at least six of them are dedicated to Extraverted Intuition.

You've got to feed the engines.

While ENTJs are driven to create control and structure, we are, quite literally, driven to do the opposite: We need change! Like a river, if the flow stops and things stagnate, we become unhealthy. Okay, technically we can feed our engine with books and classes and don't NEED to create chaos or give up control, but let's be real here...that's how ENFPs in their 80s keep sane. You start feeding your Ne with reading and crossword puzzles now and... well... it ain't going to be pretty when you're in diapers (more on that later in this chapter).

We thrive on new experiences that feed our Extraverted Intuition and ENFPs will do well to design their lives around the ability to keep their Ne satisfied. An ENFP with a structured life who tries to spice it up with some novelty, thinking salsa classes and the odd trip, will never be fully satisfied and will be living a fractional existence at best.

In the same way an ENTJ with a turbulent life will always feel unstable and be desperate to find ways to add control and certainty, an ENFP thrust into a predictable life will always feel bored and desperate to throw in uncertainty wherever they can.

Sometimes this uncertainty takes the form of an amazing romance or unforgettable trip... other times, it might take the form of manifested interpersonal drama, self-destructive behavior, or a poverty-destined career bouncy ball game.

A Gift and a Curse

I used to be envious of the ENTJs I knew in University: They were always more confident and consistent, did well in sports and competition, and after graduation thrived financially. I admired their projection of confidence and ability to handle confrontation and face down uncomfortable situations.

It's natural for ENFPs to feel this way as ENTJs thrive in the areas we sometimes struggle. Since Te, Extraverted Thinking, is their primary function it is extremely strong whereas it is our third function and therefore much weaker.

But it is a two-way street.

I remember one ENTJ friend who I admired greatly in university once said to me after a few beers, "Man, the things I could do if I had your brain."

He was alluding to the fact that I had a tremendous amount of intelligence and creativity that he saw hampered by my indecision and inconsistency...

Of course, what he didn't know is that if he had my brain, he wouldn't have the parts of his brain that allow him to be so consistent. Yes, ENTJs will eventually become jealous of our authenticity and ingenuity, and the subsequent envious lives we live... but it takes some time.

I've Got Some Good News

"A sane person to an insane society must appear insane."
—Kurt Vonnegut

According to Bronnie Ware, a nurse, when asked on their deathbed about their regrets, her patients' answers came back to five themes:

1. " I wish I'd had the courage to live a life true to myself—not the life others expected of me."

2. " I wish I hadn't worked so hard."

3. " I wish I'd had the courage to express my feelings."

4. " I wish I had stayed in touch with my friends."

5. " I wish that I had let myself be happier."

A 2018 study reached similar conclusions, finding that people were more likely to express "ideal-related regrets" such as failing to follow their dreams and live up to their full potential.

Fascinating how #1 is the theme of this book (I didn't plan it this way) and perhaps the #1 reason clients seek me out.

What about how #2 and #4 reflect the importance of relationships over material gain and status—two themes I hear over and over again from ENFPs. It seems very similar to how most ENFPs tell me they prefer spending money on experiences rather than material items or how almost all my early travel was motivated by visiting friends or family.

Might it be the case that ENFPs aren't the weird ones but are actually just connected to what it means to be human?

Perhaps our defiant nature helps us avoid falling into the societal traps of work for work's sake, buying happiness, and living in fear?

If you compare your external success to that of other people motivated by money, status, and certainty in your 20s, 30s, or 40s, you're always going to feel behind. You're always going to feel like the loser because it's a loser's game. No one wins as long as you're running on that treadmill of despair.

> You win when you see what really matters in life and design your life around it.

We didn't choose to be who we are: We are born this way. Sure, we have plenty of autonomy in how we choose to live, but if you're an ENFP, you need to feed that Ne if you want to be at your best. Fortunately for you, me, and all our ENFP family, if you feed your beast right, you can do so while living the kind of life people dream of and the kind of life you'll look back on with a big-ass grin.

I'll admit this is a ridiculous idea but thinking about what ENFPs value in comparison to how many other types live their lives while looking at that list above, one could almost conclude that it is, in fact, ***ENFPs who are the sane ones and everyone else who is fucking insane.***

Of course, this is crazy talk. It is not like there has ever been a period in history when the vast majority of people went along with the masses and did anything wrong. When you read the autobiographies of great heroes, entrepreneurs, and artists, they always emphasize how important it is to go with the herd and never challenge the status quo.

I believe it was Winston Churchill who said "Everyone just chill out! If Hitler was really such a bad guy why would all those nice German boys keep saluting him?"

And who could forget Nelson Mandela's famous proclamation, "Maybe these racist cunts are onto something and we should stay in our lane."

And, of course, one of the most famous ENFP thinkers of all time, Mark Twain, once said "If you ever find yourself questioning things or opposing the masses, it is time to pause, bury those feelings deep down, and go to law school."

Fine Wine, 90s Hip Hop, and ENFPs

What do all these things have in common? *They age extremely well.*

There are some natural phases to life that many people go through and that, in many societies, appear necessary: Education from childhood into your teens; learning who the heck you are in your 20s; building some knowledge, skills and wealth in your 30s, 40s and 50s; and enjoying the heck out of life while supporting the next generation in your 60s and beyond.

Then you start pooping yourself again.

If you follow your calling as an ENFP, you're going to have a tremendously satisfying life right up until that last point. That last point sucks for everyone... see the chapter on "the benefits of starting solo skydiving in your 80s" for alternative solutions.

The whole idea of retirement is ridiculous if you love what you do. Passionate, busy people stay healthier and live longer...at least that's what I tell myself. Also ridiculous: The idea of spending 3-4 decades of your life doing something you don't enjoy so you can one day take some cruises with other people also on the verge of pooping themselves.

We both know I could write a whole book about this but we also both know I don't need to convince you here, so let's save a tree and agree it is better to have a life of continuous pleasure, growth, and contribution than one split into two chunks:

Chunk One: Life sucks, but I bought a house, so that's cool.

Chunk Two: I have money and time, but my private parts don't work very well anymore.

Instead, I propose a life pattern that involves maximizing your life's pleasures while those private parts of yours are working fine and dandy while also building your knowledge, skills, and wealth doing something you're good at and love doing.

Then maybe when I'm old and Mr. Dan stops working so well, I'll start putting in those 60-hour work weeks.

Just kidding, Mr. Dan is never going to stop working. NEVER!

Oh god. But what if...no...is it possible?!

OK, I'm going to drop my working hours from 20 a week to 10 and ensure Mr. Dan's time on earth is maximized.

How To Live To 300

So, I think I've found both the fountain of youth and a time machine all in one.

Yes, yes, I know I probably should have led with that and added it to the book cover but I'd rather under promise and over deliver.

Let me tell you about two years of my life, starting with where I was living.

- ▶ Vancouver, Canada - January 2012
- ▶ New York - February 2012
- ▶ Costa Rica - May 2012
- ▶ New York - Summer 2012
- ▶ Vancouver, Canada - August 2012
- ▶ Hamburg, Germany - Sept 2012
- ▶ Bologna, Italy - Jan 2013
- ▶ Barcelona, Spain - April 2013
- ▶ Hamburg, Germany - Sept 2013

In addition to living in 6 countries during these two years, I also had about a dozen vacations, two epic California road trips, and fell in love somewhere between two to four times depending on if you take more of an Anglo Saxon interpretation of love or lean towards the more generous Latin American approach.

During this time, I also created DreamsAroundTheWorld.com, published my first two books, and started my coaching business.

In other words, there was a tremendous amount of moving, shaking, and lovemaking packed into these few years.

Soon after, I "settled" down in Prague. Settled is a strong word since I was still traveling a few months every year to places like Brazil, Panama, and New Zealand, but I did own a sofa, so I think settled is an accurate description. This is how I lived from 2014-2019. Relatively stable, in a loving long-term relationship, gradually growing my business.

Author's Note: This totally doesn't belong in this section, but I will just share that my overall creative juices and productivity dropped off big time when I "settled down" in one spot, then picked up again when I became more nomadic. I know this is totally counter-intuitive, but so much that works for us ENFPs is.

How Do You Measure a Life?

Instinctively we all know that some days fly by while others drag on. We all have moments where time stands still in the best sense and we've all experienced seconds feeling like hours. I'm proposing to think proactively about how you live so you can maximize your life experience and experience of time.

If you had to choose between having a life of adventure, growth, love, and new experiences... but dying in five years or living for 500 more years doing roughly the same thing every day, which would you choose?

How much of a vacation is the vacation itself versus the anticipation of it and then the memories you have afterwards?

These aren't questions I am capable of answering but I can tell you this: Those two years between 2012 and 2013 occupy a disproportionately large percentage of my memories, reflective smiles and, well, travel photos.

2014-2019 were good times by any accounts. I had an incredible girlfriend I loved like crazy, I took trips, I was doing work I loved, and... and yet... It is really hard for me to understand how it was five years of time when I compare the proportion of memories I have to the two years of 2012 and 2013.

I've started to change things up again. In 2022, I spent a few weeks in Rwanda that will always fill a disproportionately large part of my memories, a few months in Paris, and this year, 2023, I'm gearing up to go full blown traveler again for the foreseeable future.

Although I do think changing locations is the ultimate life hack to prolong your experience of life, it doesn't have to be travel for you. Whatever you do to fuel your Ne, you will ultimately be creating new experiences and challenges, and whenever you break routine, you slow time. When you're visiting a city for a few weeks, you make the most of every day. When you meet someone you know you won't see again for a while, you maximize every minute together.

There is a reason why when you talk to some people, it feels like they've lived a dozen lives and with others, it feels like, well, they've barely lived one.

Please, if you take anything from this book, let it be the need to fuel your Extraverted Intuition (Ne) and do so in a way that helps you create your own fountain of youth.

A Happy Ne = The Fountain of Youth

A Happy Ne = Your Personal Time Machine

A Happy Ne = A Life Worth Living

If you'd like some practical tips on how to have more freedom and autonomy in your life by changing how you work or creating a location independent business, you're going to love the later sections on entrepreneurship and location independence.

CAN'T I JUST BE AN ESTJ?

A few months back I read a very depressing series of comments on one of my videos that essentially said: "Being an ENFP sucks because our functions aren't the most aligned with making a good average salary in a corporate job. So I'm training myself to behave like an ESTJ so I can be successful and happy".

I think the guy might have taken my made up Mark Twain quote literally! Is there some truth in his depressed nihilistic rant?

Sure, ENFPs' and INFPs'strongest functions are not aligned with the well-paying "average jobs" of today's society.

Sure, ENFPs and INFPs, when they try and conform, don't develop properly, or are unwilling to take a risk and work in their strengths, do tend to earn less money than the average ESTJ or ENTJ.

Sure, yes, if you believe the purpose of your life is to work 40-50 hours a week at an average job to earn an average income, then being born and ENFP or INFP was pretty damn unlucky.

Fortunately, you're in luck.

IF you're an ENFP, there is no chance in hell you believe your life purpose is to work an average job for an average income.

IF you're an ENFP, then you have the wiring to take risks, defy the norms, and create a life built around your strengths.

IF these first two are true for you, then at the end of the day, you're going to have a more fun and fulfilling life than anyone striving to be well aligned working an average job.

Your Calling Is Not To Strive For Average

You better get used to some attention because you were not born to blend in. Your calling is to positively impact those around you and in doing so, increase their impact. This is your highest point of leverage.

You can follow Mr. Sad Face above and force yourself to grind like an ESTJ, but you'll never be an ESTJ. An ESTJ is often happy and satisfied grinding it out on a typical career ladder. You won't be. You may mirror their external average achievements but you'll be burning out inside. *This is an exact recipe for depression and burnout.*

> When you harness your strengths in a valuable way, you'll be rewarded, appreciated, and praised by your community. When you try and squeeze into someone else's life, you'll just be a shittier version of everyone else.

What about your personal life? What if you do earn less money than other people?

Well as an ENFP, there are two typical scenarios where you can have above average potential and yet earn a lower than average income.

Scenario One

You try and conform to other people's expectations. You go to school for something like computer science or accounting. You take a safe job your family approves of. You do your very best to fit the mold.

Until you can't anymore, so you quit. Go back to school. Try a new job your family also approves of.

You repeat this cycle for a few decades.

During the times you were actually working, you did earn around the same amount as your peers, but all those gaps, all that time going back to school or job hunting really brings down your "average" income over the years.

In the end, you spend your life frustrated, financially struggling, and disappointing nearly everyone in your life.

Scenario Two

You accept you're not like everyone else and you'd like to create a life that suits you best. You value freedom, creativity, and relationships far more than social status, security, or material possessions. So you decide to align your income production with your values. Perhaps this means a lower paid job that you love or working for yourself 20-30 hours a week.

On paper you're earning less than your friends and this bugs you, but you can't put your finger on why. Aside from feeling "behind," you're actually just as happy—if not happier—than them. You enjoy your days, your stress levels are low, and you have many wonderful relationships.

> "Your life is incredible. You live the life of someone making $500,000 a year on perhaps 10% of that".
> —A Friend to Me in 2012

How much we earn does not determine our quality of life. I could bombard you with anecdotes, statistics, and studies to prove my point here, but I don't need to because you already know what I'm saying is true.

Would you rather earn $200,000 a year at a job you hate or $100,000 a year doing something you love?

Would you rather earn $100,000 a year married to a so-so partner or $50,000 a year married to the love of your life who absolutely rocks your socks off each and every night?

Would you rather earn $50,000 a year...

Just kidding. You can't go on forever. There is, of course, a minimum income we need to earn to sustain ourselves stress-free. At some point, we'd all choose the crummy well-paying job over a cardboard box. Fortunately, this is not a decision you ever need to make.

I have had many ups and downs with my income. Reflecting over the years, I can say that many of the drops, struggles, and periods of stress came because I was trying to be someone I'm not. I tried to work a certain way entrepreneur friends said I should, or focused on earning an excess amount of money I didn't really need or care about.

Why shouldn't we just behave like an ESTJ and have an easier life?

The simple answer is *because we can't.* If it were as easy as flipping a switch, perhaps we could have a debate on the merits of a simple life focused on responsibility and community status, whether it is better to burn brighter or longer, whether one should strive to change society and culture or just contort themselves into it...

I have coached hundreds of ENFPs and I will tell you that EV-ERY ONE who has come to me with burnout was trying to fit into a job someone else wanted them to have by trying to be a personality type they weren't. This almost always means trying to live in Te like an ENTJ or ESTJ.

So all you will do by trying to conform is waste a decade of your life and deal with constant burnout. The good news is you might have some savings at the end of it. The bad news is you'll spend it all on a year or two of recovery.

ENFP Story: Jasmine

Jasmine is a Finnish ENFP in her early 30s living in Sweden. When we had our first video call, she was on a five-hour trip to acquire a rare flower, just because. Jasmine, like ENFPs everywhere, is definitely not a "normal" member of her—or any—culture.

When I interviewed Jasmine as part of the ENFP Superstar Series for ENFP Unleashed members, she liked to spend her time:

- Creating holograms of holocaust survivors
- Recording audiobooks
- Voice acting and doing voice-overs(according to IMDB, this includes movies like Harry Potter and Spider-man)
- Doing translation work (OK, this one she wasn't particularly enjoying)
- Performing in theater

> " I love castles and beautiful places and wanted to spend time there," Jasmine explained, so she also became a castle tour guide. She then decided to create entrepreneurial projects out of that, "which is where the baroque singing came from."

Jasmine then added, "Oh, right, because I had some extra time with Covid, I'm now doing a masters degree in ethnology."

You'd be right in thinking Jasmine has trouble sitting still. Born in Finland and based in Stockholm, she has also lived in Buenos Aires, Hawaii, New York City, Los Angeles, North Carolina, and Paris.

Like with many ENFPs, her need to stay busy clearly started when she was young: As a child, Jasmine performed ballet and musical theater, acted, modeled, and emceed.

Then she got into politics in her teens, interning at an EU commission before writing articles for newspapers. After high school, she totally switched gears and spent some of that acting money seeing the world while studying.

Then, because of course she did, she worked as a yoga teacher before getting into health food, juicing, real estate, and perfume testing.

If you're thinking "Oh come on, that must be everything," you're wrong. She also worked as a librarian, city guide, calligrapher, and whatever the heck she did at an auction house.

Oh, and released an album.

OK, I promise, that's it. Although I'm sure when Jasmine reads this, I'll get an email starting with "Oh, I forgot to mention when I..."

While some ENFPs email me in a panic with lists of everything they're trying to do, Jasmine was extremely content with her life. It was all by design.

> "I think in the future with everything going on in the world and how jobs are changing, I think this is the right path to take. So you don't have 'this is my job and I do this' because those jobs aren't going to exist. It's better to be a full person with qualities and experiences that you can put into any setting or any problem that needs to be solved.'"

As someone who struggles to maintain even two hobbies or projects at once, I was curious how Jasmine handled it all. She had, of course, created her own approach to organization which ran very contrary to most of the bad advice ENFPs get about discipline and sticking to a routine.

Jasmine's approach? **Constantly brainstorm new ideas for how to accomplish what she wants to do.** In other words, activate her Extraverted Intuition (Ne) and come up with an approach that excites her before getting started.

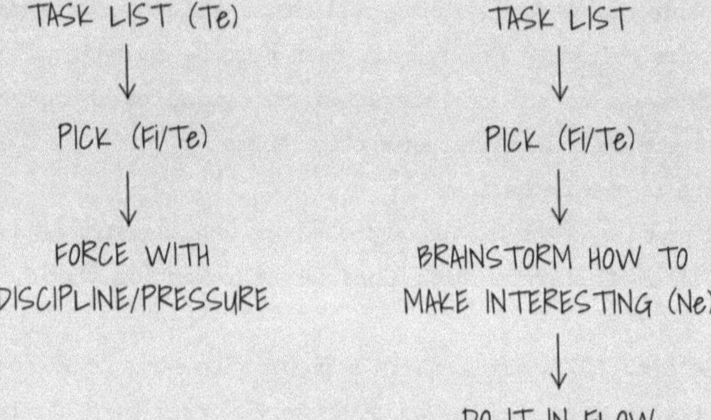

"I add an element of brainstorming to all things I have to do consistently. Whether it's cleaning or being consistent at some repetitive task I need to do, I will alter it by brainstorming around 'how can I this time, or this week, make this routine task into something exciting?' Those ideas will be endless. And that will create consistency even though I'm not experiencing it as repeating anything."

Jasmine is an incredibly inspiring example of what happens when an ENFP embraces their personality, lives life full out, and applies organizational strategies specific for ENFPs.

The full interview with Jasmine runs about an hour and is available to members of my ENFP Unleashed Program.

HOW TO READ THE REST OF THIS BOOK

Labelling the next 3 parts Relationships, Health, and Work was easy. Deciding which order I'd share them in, well, *that was hard*. I wrote this book to inspire and empower you to do something profound with your life. This was my North Star during edits and lead to many thoughts like:

"Well, for many people figuring out their life purpose, which is likely related to work, is the biggest priority right now so that should come first."

"Well, in my own life when my health has been poor I'm much less likely to make good choices around work. So it's better for people to check in with their physical and mental health before taking on their life purpose."

"Sometimes the right relationship will unlock a part of our soul and open us up to something bigger in other areas of our life. The wrong relationship could also be holding someone back."

"Yes, but perhaps once someone finds their purpose they'll be motivated to tackle their health so they can keep up and all that new energy will attract an amazing partner!"

I decided to start with relationships, followed by health, and then the largest part of this book: Your work.

For Parts 4 and 5 on relationships and health my primary focus is on improving these parts of your life so that you'll have the foundation you need to pursue your calling. At the same time, how you show up in these areas of your life is part of your calling as an ENFP.

You can read parts 4, 5, and 6 in any order you want. Do not skip around after part 6 as the rest of the book is meant to be read in order.

In what order you read the rest of the book is up to you. Most people will choose to read in the order I've laid out, but it is perfectly fine to jump around.

PLAYING WITH OTHERS

Those you invite into your life should be
a source of never ending encouragement as
you pursue your biggest dreams. You deserve
to feel loved, understood, accepted, and
appreciated in all your relationships.

Oh, and cuddles. Lots and lots of cuddles.

YOU'RE NOT THE CRAZY ONE: ON FRIENDS AND PEERS

"The thing that always attracted me to New York was the sense of being in a place where a lot of people had a lot of stories not unlike mine. Everybody comes from somewhere else. Everyone's got a Polish grandmother, some kind of metamorphosis in their family circumstances. That's a very big thing—the experience of not living where you started."
—Salman Rushdie

If you're still friends with all the people you went to high school with…
If you're living in a smaller city or town…
If you happen to have been born into a conservative country…

I'm willing to bet that the reason you often feel like people just don't get you is because you're spending time with the wrong people. This is not ideal. While I'm not going to bore you with the often cited "you're the average of the five people you spend the most time with," I will emphasize just how important your peer group is.

The only reason I've ever believed I could do more than I was doing is by meeting people who were.

Whether it was hiring a coach, joining a mastermind, or attending an event, it was by directly connecting with people who got me and were already doing something similar to what I wanted to do that I finally developed the courage to take action.

If you're working a relatively boring job, you shouldn't be surprised if your coworkers—people presumably drawn to this relatively boring job—don't seem to understand your desire to move to Cuba and teach salsa classes or start a yoga school on a sailboat. If you live in the kind of town everyone interesting leaves when they turn 18, you shouldn't be surprised if you struggle to meet anyone interesting.

Oh right, sorry. I almost forgot. Everyone is interesting in their own unique way blah blah blah. What I meant to say is that in the kind of place with a one-way migration direction, you'll likely only meet people who are interesting in the way that public radio is really interesting when you need something to help you fall asleep.

THE HUMAN MIND CAN HANDLE

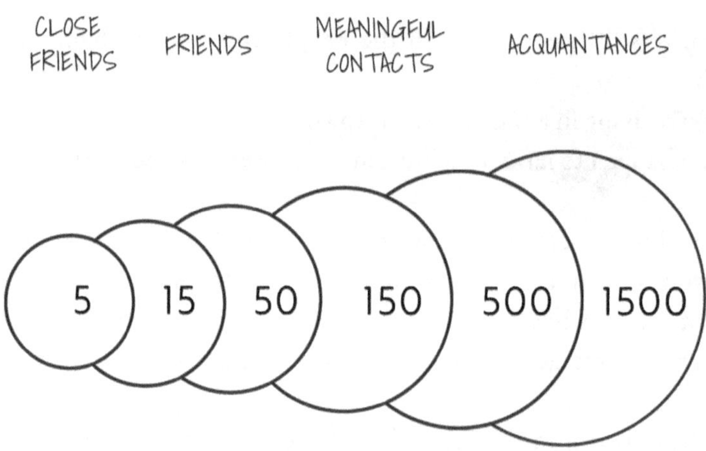

Robin Dunbar proposed we can only maintain about 150 relationships at once. Dunbar's number is illustrated above with the 5 people on the left being your closest connections. I would propose one way to improve your life is to move high quality people from the right to the left, and low quality, toxic, or unsupportive people as far right as you can.

Proactively Create Your Peer Group That

- ▸ Understands and appreciates the authentic you.
- ▸ Supports your growth.
- ▸ Is a hell of a lot of fun to hang out with.

All three are essential. Fun friends that don't support your goals or want you to be someone you aren't are a disaster. On the other hand, you'll get bored of supportive friends who aren't fun to be around.

To Build Your Peer Group

- ▸ Attend events and classes to broaden your network.
- ▸ Join things.
- ▸ Move cities. Countries. Continents if you must.

Do whatever you have to do because until you connect with people who get you, you'll never fully accept yourself, nor will you have nearly as much fun as the rest of us ENFPs are having.

> "True terror is to wake up one morning and discover that
> your high school class is running the country"
> —Kurt Vonnegut

FAMILY

"You want to get high and paint?" asked my roommate.

"Yes," I said. "Yes, I absolutely do."

 I was astonishingly confident for someone with little experience in either activity. Although as any art critic could see from my eventual masterpiece, my confidence was well founded:

13 years later and I still feel this inner conflict at times between the suited-up businessman and the artist who just wants to create or live at the beach. There have been times when I wondered what my life would be like if I grew up in Europe, or with two artists for parents, or in a hippy compound.

I grew up with two J type parents, an ESFJ and ENTJ, who loved and appreciated me and gave me plenty of opportunities to explore what I wanted to do and who I wanted to become. While they never explicitly told me what I had to do with my life, being a highly impressionable teenager, I bought into the " a good job and income is what's most important" narrative my family and culture projected.

I've accepted this was a good thing. Without that counterbalancing force of normalcy, I'd probably be that creepy old guy playing guitar in a hostel... or a best-selling novelist or famous stand-up comedian.

OK, let's not live in the past. That's takeaway #1 of this chapter. We have the parents and family we have. It is important to understand unhealthy family dynamics and work through any long-term issues these may have caused, but it is equally important to understand you're now the captain of your own ship and you have the freedom and ability to decide who you want to be and how you want to live.

OK, fine, I'll admit that being an ENFP in a family of J types can be challenging at times. One problem with J types is they think there is always a right way to do something, and naturally, they just so happen to know it. They often present this option as *the only option* as opposed to what they believe is the best option. This can lead to us ENFPs feeling like there's something wrong with us, developing a sense of shame, and trying to force ourselves into the wrong life. In some of the worst families, it's the parents or siblings locking us up, but in other cases, we end up building our own cage based on what we interpret as other people's expectations.

Kids Want To Please Their Parents

This is an important point to acknowledge: You're very capable of making assumptions about someone else's expectations for you and then creating an entire belief system and even life around this without that person ever directly telling you anything.

I haven't lived with my family for 20 years and yet their beliefs and expectations still affect me from time to time... and we've got the Atlantic Ocean between us!

If you grew up in a family that believes there is one way to live and it isn't yours, then it is going to take time and conscious effort to shake off external expectations. With time, you'll see the merit in your perspective and reap the benefits of fully embracing your personality and becoming your authentic self.

> The difference between false memories and true ones is the same as for jewels: it is always the false ones that look the most real, the most brilliant.
> —Salvador Dali

Writing Your Own Philosophy

Remember the five things people tend to regret on their deathbed?

1. " I wish I'd had the courage to live a life true to myself, not the life others expected of me."

2. " I wish I hadn't worked so hard."

3. " I wish I'd had the courage to express my feelings."

4. " I wish I had stayed in touch with my friends."

5. " I wish that I had let myself be happier."

How many of those align with the values your family shared with you as a kid? If it is more than a few, you're lucky and have some very wise parents. Few people, yes this includes our own parents, question the big-picture things such as the purpose of life. In the summer of 2022, I found myself facing an interesting situation: I was recently single, had my own location independent business and some savings, and could, well, do whatever I wanted. All expectations were open to question.

I started exploring different philosophies, primarily focused on figuring out the purpose of life... well, my life primarily. I figured I could read a few books and listen to some lectures and I'd be able to knock this one out in a few months.

Whether I discovered the absolute purpose of my life during that summer... well, we'll visit that question another time, but in the process, I discovered that just about every major school of philosophy had a different view on what life is all about.

Confucianism, which still underlies much of Chinese culture, is all about responsibility to the family and obeying authority.

Hedonists and Epicureans think life is about pleasure and happiness. The Hedonists aim to maximize pleasure while the Epicureans aim to minimize unpleasant experiences.

Socrates insists life should be lived following virtues with a high regard for legacy while Taoists aren't wasting much time contemplating what others will think after your dead.

Different times and places, different minds and faces, different answers to the same question.

During this exploration, I came across a little-known philosopher named Friedrich Nietzsche. While he had his troubles, there is no questioning Nietzsche was one of the smartest people to ever live so I was dumbfounded when I read this gem:

Nietzsche believed the purpose of life was to "Live authentically, to be creative in making your life, and to be the protagonist in your own novel."

I was taken back to journal entries and an exercise I had done in my early 20s describing what I wanted in life in almost the exact same words. This philosophy was describing how I had wanted to (and had been) living my life for years. Here was one of the most intelligent and respected philosophers in history saying the same thing.

On one hand, this brought a tremendous feeling of validation. On the other, I felt a sense of anger over the years of guilt and confusion I spent thinking something was wrong with me or that this philosophy was juvenile or irresponsible.

This brings me to the first of three guidelines for dealing with family.

Listen To Your Intuition & Find New Perspectives

This shouldn't be such a profound concept, yet for me it was. Traditionally, people were raised by an extended family if not an entire community. There were plenty of opportunities to learn about painting from Uncle Al, singing from Auntie Jacky, entrepreneurship from the neighbor down the street who owned too many jet skis.

Some people still have this. If you did, or do, be tremendously grateful. Where I grew up in Canada, I never experienced this opportunity. The neighbor who bought an RV "made the neighborhood ugly and shouldn't be allowed to park it," while the entrepreneur who decided to buy and live on a yacht was "crazy" for wasting the money. The creative people were "broke and always in trouble." When I did hear about entrepreneurial family members or neighbors, the focus was usually on money. My family, and the culture I grew up in, were great in many ways, but most often measured everything around the dollar and external success.

In my 20s I was thirsty for new perspectives and mentorship. I read every autobiography I could get my hands on, hired coaches, and took every opportunity to learn from any older person I met with some inkling of success or an interesting life. Whenever I met anyone older than me with an interesting life I'd do my best to strike up a friendship.

At some point I, like most people who go on this journey, came to the conclusion that my immediate family and the beliefs I picked up from them were likely not normal and certainly weren't universal.

I was fortunate to have always trusted my intuition about who I am and the life I want, so I was not overwhelmed with regret. Rather, I felt vindicated. I felt like "yeah, I'm not the crazy one here! My views and how I want to live my life are just as valid! Actually, according to my reading my views are likely even more valid!"

That very moment, I never heard the voice of either of my parents again, nor did the belief systems I grew up with influence a single thought, feeling, or action.

Oh man, I wish it was that easy. Unfortunately, there is often a gap or delay between awareness and changing conditioning.

This brings us to guideline #2:

If Needed, Put Some Distance Between You

For the record, I'm not planning to start a cult, so I am not encouraging EVERYONE to distance themselves from friends and family (cult recruitment tactic #5). I'm suggesting that if you feel a serious conflict between your views and the life you want and the expectations of family members or friends, then creating some physical and emotional distance for a period of time can be extremely beneficial.

In my early 20s, when I decided to invest in personal development and create my own business, I made a conscious effort to distance myself from a lot of friends and family members. Starting your own business is terrifying enough without absorbing the projected fears and anxieties of your friends in law school. That's not to say I never saw anyone, but I reduced contact and when I saw people, I tried to steer the conversation away from my own business and pursuits. As you know, I eventually moved over to Europe and added some serious physical distance although that was never the motivation behind my travels or moving.

Making a change is difficult at the best of times. It brings up a lot of vulnerabilities and fear and the last thing you want to do during this time is debate the merits of your dreams with an ENTJ who really just wants to win the argument or a well-intentioned Mom who just wants you to be "safe and happy," which means doing whatever she views as secure and mainstream.

On the other hand, we tend to love our friends and family so it would be wonderful if there was a way to maintain lots of contact while getting the space we need and pursuing life on our terms. This leads us to guideline #3

Explain Yourself and Ask for Help

Not everyone is going to listen, but you'd be surprised how responsive most people are when you are open, honest, and vulnerable while expressing what you need.

We all see life from our own perspective unless we're challenged to do otherwise. Give the people you care about a chance to understand you and see the world from your perspective and they might surprise you.

I remember having a conversation with an ENTJ friend about following the news—or, more specifically, my decision to avoid the news. He started off with something like, "That's so stupid. You're just making up random rules and overcomplicating your life."

Then I explained how the news affects me. If there is something terrible going on or an injustice in the system, I would want to fix it. Since I was not part of an elite crime fighting network it was impractical to jump around the globe righting wrongs, overthrowing dictators, and dishing out meals or vigilante justice from one day to the next.

Although, come to think of it, Che, a fellow ENFP, did cover a lot of ground in this area. I guess that's what happens when an ENFP reads the news and fully commits to making changes.

So I explained to him that reading a highly focused summary of all the wrongs and disasters in the world made me feel sad as well as helpless. It brought down my mood and limited my ability to do my own work which might, one day, put me in a position to do a lot more good around the world.

"Wow, we are so different. The news doesn't affect my mood or emotions at all. That makes total sense. If I were you I wouldn't read the news either!"

He understood.

Similar conversations can be had explaining how you're feeling sensitive or insecure about your latest creative pursuit, new business, or relationship and how you really just want support and encouragement, or to avoid the topic entirely.

Some people have trouble following orders (see Guideline #2 for dealing with them) but many will make changes for you. You may even find someone who once triggered insecurity in you becomes your biggest supporter. Maybe you're even pursuing the dream they wished they had the courage to pursue, and so they're rooting for you to succeed so they too can follow in your footsteps.

Remember that these guidelines prioritize pursuing your calling and creating the life you want. A family psychologist might give you entirely different advice if your goal is to, say, build the deepest relationship possible with your father.

I hate to throw in some self-promotion here, but I'd be doing you a disservice if I didn't mention my ENFP Unleashed Community at this point. I believe one of the fastest and most effective ways to change is by changing your peers. Hopping on a group coaching session with a dozen ENFPs from around the world is one of the fastest ways to feel, at your core, that there's never been anything wrong with you and you just needed to find your tribe.

Every major change I've made in my life started with a conversation with one or more people who opened my mind to a new way of thinking and living.

> "Parents can only give good advice or put them on the
> right paths, but the final forming of a person's character
> lies in their own hands."
> —Anne Frank

ENFP ROMANTIC RELATIONSHIPS

"Keep love in your heart. A life without it is like a sunless garden when the flowers are dead."
—Oscar Wilde
"ENFPs are gifted with the ability to bring light, joy, and pleasure to many. When it comes to relationships one could argue it is our calling to brighten the lives of those we meet, and whether that meeting is for a few hours or a lifetime, to leave each person we touch better for having met us."
—Me, but I wanted to make it into a quote.

I gave some thought as to how to approach this chapter as these days, any discussion around men and women, or gender in general, can be a touchy one, especially for those in Canada and the USA. I'd be doing you a great disservice if I were to hold back advice or speak in vague politically correct terms in an attempt to avoid any criticism. So I will be speaking about men and women and about masculine and feminine traits and energy.

I feel comfortable speaking about some near universals here because I'm drawing on an extremely wide range of experiences. From my psychology degree and classes on relationships and human sexuality at a top University to dating people from dozens of countries and cultures. I also know I'm writing for an intelligent and nuanced audience.

Remember, when anyone speaks of patterns and preferences, it is just that. Dutch people are taller than Spanish people. Yes, I know there are short Dutch people and tall Spanish people but there is a reason beds in Spain are usually 190cm long and 200cm in the Netherlands. If I'm selling jeans, I'm going to go bankrupt if I send the same proportion of sizes to Spain and the Netherlands.

Similarly, I could say women prefer a proactive take-charge man over someone indecisive or apathetic. Does this mean there aren't women who prefer a passive guy? Of course it doesn't... but if you were to ask 100 women about their preferences, the vast majority are going to choose a take charge man over Mr. Indecision.

This is a particularly relevant example because an indecisive ENFP woman can be seen as whimsical, spontaneous, and very feminine whereas that same energy in an ENFP man can come across as unsure, unreliable, and unattractive.

Don't worry guys, there is hope... actually, there's a lot of it.

Turns Out We're Hella Sexy

There was an informal internet survey done a few years ago that asked each personality type which types they were attracted to. Every single type (including ENFPs) voted that they were attracted to ENFPs.

So, how do I put this without offending all the other types...

Let's just say when it comes to romantic relationships, you've got some options and there is absolutely no reason to settle.

In fact, it is rare for an ENFP to have any trouble meeting people. Male or female, ENFPs are attractive to whoever it is they want to attract. ENFP men can struggle when we're younger and come off as too indecisive and flaky. I learned this lesson the hard way: Not many women are attracted to a guy who plans a date with, "well I dunno, what do you want to do?"

Yet with time if we're able to develop our confidence and act decisively, ENFP men can become extremely attractive. Our diverse interests, spontaneous spirit, and love of deep conversations makes us a breath of fresh air for bored women everywhere.

ENFP women often epitomize what it means to be feminine in the classical sense. They can be fun and playful, sexy and spontaneous, self-aware and mysterious, all wrapped into one incredibly provocative package.

This is very good news because many ENFPs are drawn to a life of variety and adventure and the last thing we'd want is to settle down with the first person who will give us the time of day just because we don't have any other options.

The majority of this section will be focused on the things you can do to be even more attractive as an ENFP so you can have as many dating options as you'd like as well as ways to filter out partners that are more likely to weigh you down than lift you up. This will give you the freedom to design your perfect romantic life and, if you choose, to find a partner who shares similar values.

> Your ideal partner will support you in living out your calling and having as many adventures as you'd like along the way.

For ENFPs, Our Calling Comes First

Why have a relationship at all? At first it sounds ridiculous, but it is a fair question. These days, when all our supposed needs can be met via delivery and digital content, why go through all the trouble of not only meeting other people but perhaps building something with one or more people?

Everyone knows life is better when shared, but how and why we choose to share it varies tremendously.

For example, we all know that person who *needs* to be in a relationship. They always have been and always will be. Some don't like to be alone, some like the status of having a boyfriend or girlfriend, some just don't do so well socially and find a relationship to be the only way to find companionship and sex.

Call me a hopeless romantic, but these all seem like terrible reasons to spend even a portion of your life with someone.

Then there are the couples that work so well. Together they grow and with each other, both become better people. This is what we call a relationship worth having! If you want to have a relationship, this is what you're aiming for.

On the other side are those who reluctantly accept living life alone due to some kind of block, often caused by events in their past. Deep down they'd love a vibrant dating life and, perhaps, a long-term partner, but they're not willing to do the inner and practical work required for them to do this... so they normalize a life alone, often even adopting new belief systems to justify it all.

Relationships & Your Calling

I believe most ENFPs would be better off being single than existing in a mediocre relationship and I also believe ENFPs are extremely capable of finding an incredible partner and creating a one-in-a-million relationship full of love, growth, and yes, even adventure!

My focus is on helping you understand and utilize your greatest gifts, to live out your calling, and to have the greatest positive impact possible. With the right relationship(s), you will grow exponentially, whereas the wrong partner can throw you into a holding pattern for decades.

So we are going to look at relationships through this lens: An ENFP will be at their best when they have healthy, vibrant relationships, including intimate ones, and feel the support and trust needed to fully embrace their personality and pursue their calling at the highest level.

> Of course, don't forget that part of your calling is also to
> inspire your partner and be a source of good and growth
> in all your relationships, romantic or otherwise.

What Makes ENFPs Different

ENFPs can build trust and create a deep connection with someone in a very short period of time. This is a tremendous gift and it lends itself to us having a wide impact on the world. Some types, such as INFJs, are slow to develop a connection. INFJs like to focus and go deep with one person. ENFPs like to connect with many people.

It is from this standpoint that I say: For most ENFPs, I do not believe being a monogamous partner or "the supportive parent" is our highest calling *in relation to other types.*

I'm not making any claim about whether or not ENFPs should get married or have children. Nor do I believe they shouldn't. ENFPs can be fantastic parents and partners.

What I am saying here is that I believe you will be happiest if you design your relationships and possible family around the life you want, your calling, and the impact you want to have. A thriving ENFP is a happy and fulfilled ENFP and a happy and fulfilled ENFP will be a much better partner and parent.

I believe any relationships you choose to have—and personally, I hope there will be many and you'll enjoy the hell out of all of them—should first and foremost bring you joy, support your personal growth, and move you towards self-actualization.

Remember that informal survey from the start of the chapter? Yeah... you're in the driver's seat. Everyone wants to date you, so why not take the time to think about what you really want to proactively design it?

For practical reasons, I am breaking the next sections into advice for ENFP women and men separately, but whatever your gender, you will likely find value and personal insights from each section. Why do I even need to divide things? Well, it turns out it is different to date as a man versus a woman. SHOCKING, I know. Even in the most progressive cultures, between two equally attractive people, men still are much more likely to be the one initiating, putting himself out there, risking rejection, and hoping for the best. As the ones being pursued, women have a different experience and different things to watch out for than a man, who has to work on himself to be a capable pursuer.

If you're not convinced, consider this one statistic: On online dating apps like Bumble or Tinder, women on average swipe ONE time for every SIXTY times a man swipes. In most cultures, a woman focuses on attracting the best men and then screening until she finds Mr. Right. A man strives to become one of those men that woman actually want—to become that 1 of 60.

THE LION, THE EAGLE, AND THE CAGE

> "She and I both felt it. When we left our boyfriends, it was like this weight was lifted. The light returned. We started to feel like our true selves again and regain our love and zest for life"
> —A 25-year-old ENFP describing her and her
> 31-year-old friend's recent experiences ending long-term relationships

Do not settle and do not be with anyone who dims your light. As an ENFP, you're everything anyone worth his salt dreams of. You can be fun, playful, radiant, witty, and able to bring adventure and new experiences to whomever you choose. You're also likely to be self-aware, intelligent, and a wonderful conversationalist. Word on the street is you might also be pretty good in the ol' bedroom Olympics...

So why the hell would you ever settle?

Feminine energy, of which the ENFP has plenty, is about change and possibilities. Masculine energy, which is most concentrated in the TJ types, seeks to bring structure, certainty, and control to whatever it touches. The masculine is drawn to the whimsy of the feminine, yet for some perverse reason wants to lock it up.

It is no different than picking a beautiful flower from the garden only for it to die or locking a majestic creature in a zoo to become decoration. The wrong relationship extinguishes the light which shines so bright within each ENFP. The right relationship blows oxygen on the flame and sees us burn hotter and shine brighter.

Find the partner who will love and nurture your flame. You deserve the partner who sits back and watches you cast your light with a beautiful smile upon his or her face, in awe, in full appreciation of your gifts.

The Problem with J Types

The ENFP is a more feminine personality type, which is of course magnified in ENFP women. This means a wonderful level of change, adventure, and exploration. When we push this exploration and instability too far we can create a desire for stability.

When we are enveloped in change and uncertainty, when we're unable to rely on ourselves to be consistent for a time, such as when we hit a rough spot of intense stress or a few failures in a row, we will crave external structure and certainty. This reaction is normal: Without a leash, how does the eagle not fly away and burn up in the sun? To which the wrong partner says, what about a cage to keep it from flying at all?

We think we want the leash but what we really want is a perch we know we can return to. A perch that will be secure and welcoming. With this perch we can feel free to fly as far and wide as we'd like without fear of losing ourselves.

It is commonly understood that the best long-term partners for ENFPs are introverted J types. You may have heard that INTJs and INFJs are ideal.

It is also very common for ENFP women to end up dating ESTJ or ISTJ men because their stability and certainty can be appealing, especially if the couple meets at a time of chaos or change for the woman.

And this is where the potential for caging can come in. ENFPs are extremely open and adaptable. The P in our personality lends itself to an open and adaptive way of structuring ourselves and the world. When asked what is most important in life, what is right or wrong, what one should do, an ENFP will often contemplate possibilities and use open language, words such as "perhaps," "often," "maybe," "for me right now," etc.

Many J types are different. They have a clear structured world view. They have no problem stating how they or someone else should live. They are often clear about what they want, or at least they believe they are.

Well, what happens when water collides with stone? Of course it is the water that adapts and changes direction, not the stone. The water may notice the stone start to erode: a sharp edge curves, a course surface smooths... but make no mistake, while the stone will benefit from the water's polishing, it has no intention of going anywhere and will always be a stone.

What about a river of water so intense it flows for miles, moves boulders, and polishes every stone it touches? Well, let me ask you: What interest should such a river have in any one little stone? A mountain perhaps, but then we're back to square one, aren't we?

So it is the ENFP who often feels the need to change and adapt to the ways of their J partners. They're made to feel guilty for their energy and love of novelty... there is something wrong with your way of being that must change to be a good girlfriend, boyfriend, partner, spouse, or parent.

If an ENFP has parents who also imparted this kind of guilt and shame for their way of being, it is almost certain they'll find themselves caged by a partner.

Understand: The ENFP Cage

ENFPs can be incredibly seductive and desirable. For most, we are a breath of fresh air and an invitation into a world of fantasy, adventure, and pleasure that most rarely experience. This makes us very attractive in the early stages of a relationship... but what about after that?

What happens when the novelty of our partner begins to wear off and we no longer put in the same effort to seduce we once did? What happens when our charm diminishes or our once unpredictable and alluring nature becomes routine?

For the wrong person, some of the traits that make us most appealing in the romantic stages of courtship can be terribly annoying in a long-term relationship. Someone looking for a stable vanilla relationship may initially be drawn to the excitement they feel around us with the naive assumption that they'll be able to reign us in, or that one day we'll grow up, settle down, or in whatever other way, fit their expectations for a "grown up life."

Now our partner sees our spontaneity as disorganized, our romanticism as an immature distraction, our idealism as unrealistic.

They want to cage the lion.

When caged, the lion loses its charm. Now, not only are we feeling caged, criticized, and unappreciated—we're also not nearly as appealing to our partners as we once were. In a rational world we'd already be planning our escape, but human nature often means adapting to our situation and embracing a cage over the uncertainty of an uncomfortable conversation or big life change.

Takeaway: Watch out for future jailers. Probe your date's future dreams and desires. If they're too predictable, too vanilla, get out while you can. If they're looking to insert someone into their clear and certain life plan, run. **It is much easier to cage an eagle than train a goat to fly.**

Another Look: What if you find yourself with a partner who loves certainty, but you want to stay together? How can you make it work?

Reconnect with your real personality and bring your soul back alive. Seduce them all over. If you can maintain the soul and spirit they first fell in love with, you can direct their attention away from minor annoyances and instead to why they first fell in love with you. Rekindle the romance and adventure and you can get away with forgetting to pay the heating bill.

DATING TIPS FOR THE ENFP ON THE PROWL

Of any part of this book, this next section is most based on my personal experience and one-on-one conversations with both men and women from around the world. Some statements may be controversial or sound outdated, but my advice wouldn't be helpful if I didn't write what was true.

There have been times in my life when I've run into a dating struggle and turned to the internet for answers. Always a terrible idea.

Whether articles on mainstream magazines or posts on Reddit, I quickly realized I was almost always reading people who didn't have a clue what they were talking about. Or worse, someone writing an article on dating based on dogma and ideology versus experience and reality.

My own experience reaches across a wealth of cultures. I've been in meaningful relationships with women from five of the seven continents. Damn you Australia and Antarctica... one day I'll meet my dream penguin. I ask a lot of questions, often really simple, seemingly dumb ones like, "Why do you like me?" or "What do you look for in a man?"

So, here are a few things I've learnt from my research.

Embrace Your Right to Freedom and Choice

There are 16 personality types. 16 of them think ENFPs are awesome. You're the boss. If you grew up in a small town without many options or had experiences that brought down your self-confidence, work on this before "settling down." You deserve the best and are capable of having it. This is doubly true if you're planning to have kids. You'll do you and your future rug rats a huge service by becoming your best self before picking that forever partner.

Learn To Play Detective

Fine-tune your intuition and learn to observe the details. You'll naturally see the best in people, but before going too far, like having 7 kids, you'll want to put on your bad cop hat and look for flaws and future trouble. Sometimes it is helpful to get another perspective from a friend or family member who is in a healthy relationship themselves and whose opinion you respect. Whether or not you agree with their assessment, it will give you something to reflect on.

Seek Appreciation and Expansion

Some people will appreciate your gifts, see your potential, and nourish your soul. These people will help you grow and self-actualize. Be with these people.

Break Cultural Barriers

I'm fortunate to have met ENFPs from dozens of cultures and countries. ENFP women from traditional families and cultures, especially Muslim majority countries, have a tough deal. If you find your intuition telling you your family's or culture's conservative expectations of you are unfair, limiting, or just plain wrong, consider making a move. See my tip below, Location Matters.

On the other hand, perhaps you live somewhere going through a period of hyper-progressivism and you'd like to date a guy or gal who is a little more traditional. Perhaps you appreciate a little romance and still like the idea of flowers and door holding. Once again, if your intuition tells you the culture around you is wrong, or wrong for you, don't ignore that feeling. Be true to yourself.

There have always been people telling us how we're supposed to feel, what we're supposed to like, and how we're supposed to behave. The sheer variety and turbulence of these doctrines is proof enough that none are—or ever were—"correct" for everyone, or perhaps anyone, and billions of people have suffered as a result of this repression. Yet, there have always been brave people who trusted their own intuition above others and did what was right for them.

Learn To Dance

Courtship is a two-way dance. If you'd like to attract an amazing mate you must practice being attractive.

"Just be yourself and if he doesn't like you for you, it's his loss," is terrible advice. Don't believe me? Just ask all the men testing the theory by having a lame job, making Family Guy jokes, and playing Call of Duty 40 hours a week. How many women are lining up to date them?

Dancing teaches us how to be one part of a whole, how to connect with another person, and how to play our part in something bigger than us. It also teaches you how to flirt and play your part in seduction.

Role Models

We are all influenced by the outside world. Choose your influences and you can choose who you'll become.

Become The Person Your Ideal Partner Wants

> Women aren't attracted to money. They're attracted to men who are free and captains of their own ship. Ask 100 women who they would rather date: An obedient middle manager at a tech company earning $150k a year or a passionate entrepreneur or artist earning $60k who is happy, self-aware, confident, loves what they do, and answers to no one?

When I was in my early 20s, I hired a coach to help me improve my life. One session, I was telling her about my experience at a bar. I asked her what I could have said or done to meet this incredible woman I'd seen.

My coach was clear: "Don't think about what to say or do to be with her. Think about the type of man she wants to be with. Become that man."

Interestingly, this aligns with one of my core beliefs around business: To focus your time on proactive, asset-creating activities.

Develop your emotional intelligence, find your calling, spend your time doing things that really matter. Be a great friend and family member, make the world a better place, make your word matter, and do the things you say you're going to.

> Instead of wasting your days on dating apps, invest your time in becoming the type of person your ideal partner would drool over. Of course, do this within reason and while being true to your personality.

Like sports? Become a great athlete. Like music and dance? Become a musician or excellent dancer. Like to paint? Become a great painter. This tip isn't about external accomplishments—that is coming up but we often develop internally during the pursuit of something external.

Takeaway: Spend 80% less time swiping and texting and invest that time in becoming the man they'll be chasing.

Practical Steps:

- Take Dance Classes
- Learn a Language
- Develop Your Personality, Self-Awareness, and Confidence
- Travel
- Do Something Creative
- Start a Business

Author's Note:

I know the above tip can easily be confused with becoming fake or changing yourself in an unhealthy way to meet someone else's expectations. It is not meant in this way because ultimately your mind will create an image of what your perfect partner wants that is actually your own ideal for yourself...which is a very good thing to strive for.

We are all changing and shaping ourselves based on external pressures whether or not we know it or are honest enough to acknowledge it. I'm only advocating you take charge of this and do it proactively towards a vision you create as opposed to the vision created by ad agencies, governments, families etc.

Your True Self Is Your Most Attractive

People love authenticity and confidence. Be happy, be spontaneous, be your true self, and you'll never have a shortage of dates.

Location Matters

Location matters tremendously for dating. It's easy to understand that if you like tall, pale men, Sweden might be your jam. If you like short, tanned men with an athletic approach to love making, Brazil might be your spot. You'll find massive differences in people, personalities, and dating culture between cities, countries, and continents.

As much as my romantic soul hates to say it, there is a geographic and economic basis to dating.

Whether it is changing cities, countries, or continents, consider moving to a place that has a culture and people more aligned with your values and the type of people you'd like to date.

ENFP Story Sena

Sena, a gynecologist living in France, is walking proof that no matter how hard the world tries to hide it, there is a powerful energy within every ENFP waiting to come out.

I first spoke to Sena about attending Life Design Fiesta in Prague. She was pretty clear that she wanted to get out of a relationship she just couldn't shake off after years. A situation not helped by a conservative family.

Sena wanted to feel free and to regain that same belief in herself that once empowered her to move to France on her own and, against her family's wishes, become a gynecologist.

On day four of the event, Sena shared, " I sent my friend a photo of me yesterday. She said 'What happened?! Your light has returned. Your smile is back. You're back!'"

It was obvious to everyone. The Sena who sat in front of us on day four was not the Sena who arrived on day one.

Sena was one of the test readers for this book, and we often exchange messages. Her specialty is sending photos of her radiant smile from exotic locations, most recently in South America. Referring to ending her relationship and making a life change, I remember someone saying to her, " it's a little crazy you came to an event just to help you do something you knew you needed to do."

Sena replied, "It wasn't just the event. It was over a year of therapy and all sorts of other work I paid for."

I'm grateful Sena got what she needed from the event, was finally able to embrace who she always was, and made the big changes she knew were needed. I'm not surprised: For us ENFPs, often all we need is a few days with people like us, who get us, to remind us who we really are and what we really want.

The ENFP Infatuation

"Oh, so I'm flighty, flaky, changing my mind... maybe I did learn something"
—Michael Scott

Me in my 20s, from my 2013 book:
"ENFPs can be overly enthusiastic. In the early stages of a relationship, avoid making gushy or smothering comments during the moments you just happen to feel something strong.

You may turn some partners off, and you may give other partners unrealistic expectations about how strongly you feel for them."

Me in my 30s, in this book:

"Fuck it, life is short and if there was ever a time we needed some romance, it's now. If in that moment you can't imagine a happiness greater than the touch of her hand on yours, tell her, hold her, kiss her."

A few months ago, it hit me: I had starved my romantic soul. I really don't know if it was from taking my own advice or a natural byproduct of aging, but I had tapered down my expression of, and therefore my experience of, my romantic feelings.

I had taken on a ridiculous belief that if I don't know how I'll feel the next week, I shouldn't express a feeling today. That if I know I'm not keen on a long-term relationship, I shouldn't show affection because someone could be disappointed.

That's stupid.

As long as I am honest and authentic, I'm not responsible for other people's feelings and I am definitely not responsible for the ridiculous paradigm that romance, affection, and passion can only be expressed within a long-term relationship.

So I said "to hell with it" and just started letting my heart sing again, and wow—wow, has it been an amazing few months.

Make People's Lives Better

> "Every true lover knows that the moment of greatest satisfaction comes when ecstasy is long over and he beholds before him the flower that has blossomed beneath his touch."
> —Don Juan DeMarco

I've always had some conflicted feelings about how to date given my love of travel and movement.

Living in and visiting so many places has given me tremendous insights into human nature. Naive little 18-year-old Dan, buying into dated stereotypes and beliefs we learned in Canada, would have assumed no woman would be interested in a man visiting for only a week or two. Oh how wrong I was.

Early in my travels I came up with this idea: When I meet someone, do my best to be a good part of their life.

I know it's simple: All good guiding principles should be.

I think I've done a decent job sticking to this. Over my years I've collected some pretty inspiring stories, including my pillow talk inspiring a best-selling erotic fiction novelist and being the catalyst for at least a few loves and marriages.

People don't always need a soulmate to awaken their soul; sometimes a kiss, some loving words, or a moment of deep caring and support is enough.

Okay, I'm going to be practical here. If you're enjoying your single life and don't want to burn in hell, here are a few keys:

- Minimize lying.
- Cuddle, be kind, be open, and learn how to make a nice breakfast.
- Never ghost anyone you've been close with. Ghosting is the most cowardly and pathetic thing a person can do.
- Use your ENFP powers of seeing the best in people. Make your dates feel special and appreciated. Show them how awesome they are.

These 3 Are Just For The Men

How many of you were offended when I said we have a feminine personality?

Come on, let's be honest. Sure I'm 6'4, have a beard, and like action movies, but my favorite thing to do is talk about psychology and emotions, I love dramatic relationship-driven shows, and I'm quite sure the moon might actually affect my emotions.

I've come to terms with having many feminine elements to my personality and I need to be honest here...

As I get older, it has been treating me very well on the ol' dating market. It turns out, in a world devoid of romance and ripe with dry conversation, rigid thinking, and the same ol', same ol', we ENFP guys are pretty damn popular.

Well, at least we have the potential to be. I hope these next 3 insights will help you along your way.

Be Decisive

Or at least fake it. Indecision is a libido killer. No one is attracted to an indecisive man.

This is a bit of an issue for us ENFP guys because, well, we are wired for indecision. I can take hours to choose a restaurant for lunch.

It is absolutely essential you take charge and plan the first few dates. If you happen to meet a more decisive take-charge woman and she suggests a place, awesome. No need to assert yourself. But most women are going to lean on you to suggest the plan of action for the date.

You could plan a unique and magical date each time... but given our tendency to overthink, I would suggest you take an hour and plan out around five good first dates and repeat them. It isn't about what you do; it's about who you do it with.

This same decisiveness goes for how you act on the date. If you feel a connection and you know you're going to kiss your date, the best time to do it is any time except at the very end of the date. Nothing says "I've been too scared to kiss you all night" than a last-minute kiss when the taxi is literally honking at her.

Embrace that ENFP impulsiveness. When you feel a moment, when your eyes meet and she gives you that look, just kiss her. The more awkward or uncomfortable the situation (e.g., a crowded place), the more romantic it is that you chose to kiss her right then. The higher the risk of public rejection, such as when people all around will see it, the more confidence it shows when you do it.

Damn, I can't believe I'm including this. These are the tips I don't even share with my close friends.

Watch Out For: Never feel the need to force your choices on people or be overly assertive. You're not trying to be a 1950s so-called Alpha Male. Just learn to be decisive enough to keep your dates interested and save yourself from hours of anxiety and overthinking.

Accomplish Things. It Matters

Women do not like to date down. Don't believe me? Look up any dozen famous and successful men and compare their career achievements and social status to their wives. Do the same with a dozen successful women.

A successful woman wants a successful man. An intelligent woman wants an intelligent man. An ambitious woman wants an ambitious man. *Oh, and they all know many men are full of shit and will say just about anything to charm them.* This means they look at your accomplishments as a trustworthy indicator of your traits, who you really are, and what kind of partner you'll be.

Nice Physique = Discipline
Work Success = Work Ethic, Intelligence
Volunteering = Kindness, Generosity
Lots of Friends = Social, Loyal, Well Liked

I have always been a hopeless romantic. When I was in my teens and early 20s, I was also a *naive* hopeless romantic. I truly believed women did not, even a little, care about a man's body or financial success. I thought life was all Disney movies, where a look and a connection, true love, was all that mattered.

I'm embarrassed to admit it really took me until my mid-30s to notice that all the princes in Disney movies are buff, handsome, rich, and powerful.

Be a hopeless romantic AND develop your personality, get good at things, and do something that matters with your life.

"Dan, you really are the stupidest smart person I've ever met."
—My Italian Friend Davide

Don't Lie

An ENFP with an underdeveloped Fi might read the above tip on accomplishing things and think: *Perfect, I just need to say I've done important things.*

No! BAD DOG.

I hate those guys. Firstly, because lying is a douchebag move. Secondly, because when I tell women I'm an author and entrepreneur, they roll their eyes. Apparently, it's a common lie guys tell when visiting Europe.

Although I must admit, I don't mind that you're making it harder for me. It pushes me to improve.

This is exactly why you should never lie about your accomplishments. Lying about who you are will take you down a terrible hole which is incredibly hard to climb out of. Wanting the feelings and rewards that come from accomplishments is a priceless source of motivation. In chasing after a dream you'll be forced to confront demons, develop your personality, and become the kind of person who accomplishes their dreams.

It is not the accomplishments that people are attracted to or that make you feel good; it is the person you become during the journey that make you attractive. Becoming and being this person is what feels great. When you skip the transformational step, you rob yourself of a great gift, and once you begin lying, it is incredibly tough to go back.

ENFP Relationships TLDR: Never Settle

For most ENFPs, a bad relationship is much worse than no relationship. We are much better off being single, meeting many people, and growing and exploring than being in a relationship that could cage or limit us. Yet it is possible to create a relationship that will provide the love, support, and growth opportunities that can make us and our lives even better.

These kinds of relationships are rare but fortunately, ENFPs are very desirable extroverts with a passion for the kind of personal development and work suited for creating such an amazing relationship once we've met the right person.

So if anyone can find the perfect partner and create the right relationship, it's an ENFP. Yet, if there is a type that's more than capable of living a vibrant, fulfilling life full of many relationships and connections instead of settling down with that one "for life" person, it's also an ENFP.

ENFP SUPERPOWERS

THE MINER

"Do you mind if I undo my pants?"
—My Mother

Yes, this is how my parents met. On a flight back from India, my mom was upgraded to business class where she was seated beside my dad. She dropped this gem of a pickup line and the two were married five weeks later.

Nether are ENFPs, but I'd like to think their meeting, my origin story, sure is.

When confident and comfortable in their own skin, ENFPs can be tremendously open and trusting and create these same feelings in those we meet. We're the "wow, it feels like I've known you forever" type.

This allows us to skip the small talk and jump into deep conversations and meaningful relationships a lot faster than most everyone else. Sure, there are risks to this, but as a strength, it is invaluable.

Potential Superpower: Skipping the small talk, making meaningful connections, and deepening relationships.

Blocks: People can't be comfortable with you if you aren't comfortable with yourself. They won't trust you if you don't trust yourself.

Keys To Developing: Being the most confident, authentic and self-loving version of yourself will help maximize this superpower. In addition, develop your intuition and learn to open up and share the right amount of vulnerability. Too much and you come off as a weird over-sharer, too little and you come off as closed and miss out on the opportunity to develop more open and meaningful relationships.

Watch Out For: One reason we're able to do this is because we really are open and trusting. As one ENFP client said to me, "It never occurs to me that someone might actually be lying to me."

Over time, you'll develop your intuition. Across nearly 50 countries and thousands of people, I've had, perhaps, two to three bad experiences. If you're young or if you come from a small town, when you're meeting someone new, spend a few minutes playing bad cop and deciding if the person you're with deserves your trust.

ENFP SUPERPOWER

THE STORYTELLER

Do you want to hear a story? Of course you do. Listening to a great story is one of life's greatest joys and few are able to tell one.

You, my friend, have the wiring to be one of the few, but this superpower must be developed.

You have likely racked up a collection of stories to go along with your charming spontaneity, impulsiveness, and downright insanity... and that's step one.

Step two is learning how to tell a story.

Potential Superpower: To become a captivating storyteller and be the most entertaining date, party guest, or salesperson.

Blocks: A lack of self-awareness or a big ego will block this. Look around, pay attention to the reaction of your audience, and speak with the intention to bring joy and not to impress.

Keys To Developing: Listen to great storytellers. Read books. Watch well-written shows. Practice telling the same story a few times with a few variations on how you tell it until you get things right. Many stand-up comedians tell a joke 10, 50, 100+ times before they find the precise wording that makes it a hit.

ENFP SUPERPOWER

THE EXPERIENCE CREATOR

Some people are surprised by how rarely I visit Canada. They're astonished that I don't prioritize going back to Canada for a few weeks every year. As anyone who lives abroad knows, when you visit home, you often just slot yourself into the boring routines everyone else is up to.

I'd much rather create an experience and new memories abroad with one of my parents or brother than go home for a few weeks of highly forgettable meals and small talk.

Since leaving Canada, I've traveled with my mom to Panama, Italy, Prague, Germany, Croatia, Bosnia, Serbia, Montenegro, and Romania.

My brother and I spent two weeks in Costa Rica together as well as visiting Germany, Spain, Malta, Berlin, and Vienna on an epic 17-day trip.

While I will admit my mom did most of our travel planning together, I LOVED planning the trips for my brother and giving him these experiences.

I don't see my friends in Prague quite as often as I'd like, but I do throw some of the best parties: Halloween, New Year's Eve, summer BBQs... I love bringing people together and creating experiences for them.

I know I'll never be that perfect son or friend who calls every day for a 30-minute chat but what I can do is give value in all my relationships by creating special experiences.

So can you.

Potential Superpower: Creating unforgettable experiences.

Blocks: It's really just a matter of effort. Be careful of overplanning, which might lead to overthinking every little detail. Instead, come up with a general idea and trust your ability to make an experience fun and memorable in your spontaneous way.

Keys to Developing Practice makes perfect. Just do it.

HEALTH, ENERGY, AND FOCUS

You have the ability to feel clear, confident, and energized. If you're going to be fulfilling your calling and acting as a force for good you need to be at your best physically and mentally so you can deliver at your highest potential. You owe it to yourself and the world.

Also, I heard you're going to have one heck of an amazing life so might as well make it long right? I want to hear all the stories.

Queue the Rocky Montage music.

GOING FOR GOLD

How to Waste A Perfect Day

While some believe life is too short, others prefer to waste as many days as possible and get the whole mess over with.

Fortunately for you, I used to be an absolute master of wasting my days and really perfected the entire process. Now I offer you a personalized guide to wasting what could have been a perfect day. You may implement this advice at any time, but I found it has a near 100% success rate when applied after a large lunch. Specifically, the one-two punch of eating a huge lunch and then sitting down on the sofa to consume mindless content for "just a few moments to rest" is guaranteed to work.

This is my own recipe to ruin your days, weeks, and quite possibly, if you really apply yourself, your entire life. But don't limit yourself and feel free to create your own formula for life destruction.

It starts with something you want to do. A vague, foggy idea works best—nothing too clear, or it will mess things up because you might actually accomplish something. A daily goal like " I want to work on my website today" or "I'm going to work on my book" is great.

If you can't pinpoint one thing, you can always just open your inbox and stack up a dozen small requests and problems by reading all your emails and not responding. Load up your mind with those unaddressed decisions!

Next, you need to double down on your intuition and ponder every possible option and outcome. Be sure to do this in your head, and only in your head. Writing things down, or even speaking out loud, could make things too clear or break the pattern.

Next up, you want to jump from one possibility to the next without making any decisions or even narrowing down your options. Ideally, you want to bring in even *more* options and criteria. Really load it on.

Now—and this is important—you have to get your body into the right position. It's likely you're already a bit worn down and low on cognitive energy, but that isn't always enough. If you go for a walk or even just stand tall, you risk breaking the pattern. It's essential that you adopt the fetal position. My personal favorite location for this is the sofa, but a rug or dog house will suffice in a pinch.

If you're not experienced enough to go full fetal, a backup solution is anything horizontal and sloth-like. Running back to bed and stretching out will do.

Now, at this stage you've depleted every last drop of cognitive energy. You were already running low; the best time to master this is mid-afternoon. Spending even fifteen minutes doing non-stop analysis of multiple outcomes is usually enough to polish off the last of your reserves.

This is where the grand finale comes in. While you sloth away, drained of mental energy, you must keep your eye on the prize. This is where many mess up, break the funk, and actually accomplish something.

Resist the urge to get up. Do not walk to the other room. Do not call a friend or colleague. That would break your train of thought. No matter what, do not even *think* about doing jumping jacks or taking a walk! That will dismantle everything you've been working so hard to accomplish.

To complete your finale just take it out. No, not that, Louis. Take out your *phone*. Just kidding; if you've made it this far, I'm sure you've already been spending most of your day staring at your phone. So keep it out and start the scroll. Instagram, Twitter, BBC News... whatever you prefer. You're the boss! If you really want to destroy your life, be sure to download TikTok!

Let the scrolling begin.

If you're lucky, you live alone and don't have any accountability built into your work or business. This will give you a straight shot to sundown.

Alright, now time for some bonus points.

Some people shake themselves off around sunset. Feeling they may not have invested their time quite as effectively as they would have liked, they eat a healthy dinner and go to bed early so they can start fresh tomorrow.

But you're not some people. You're special. You're aiming for rock bottom and this is where you take your stand. This is where you shine.

There is no way you're going to risk resting up and having a better tomorrow.

Gather up all the guilt you're feeling from your day. Really squeeze it all out. Don't miss a drop. Now channel this guilt into a few pizzas, a tub of ice cream, or a six-pack. Or... oh, what the heck, let's do all three! You're no quitter. Load up a Netflix series and set your sights on 3 a.m.

You got this!

When we break it down, it's really quite comical, but it's easy to fall into this pattern.

Some habits are more important to break than others. My top tip would probably be to stop checking your phone in bed. If you can't stop doing *all* these things, you'll still make progress if you at least stop doing *some* of them.

Or, you know, you can be a real champion and waste your whole life in a mess on the sofa. #winning...

If, at the very least, you recognize your *choice* to do that, and to engage in all of these habits, then you'll start to hold yourself accountable sooner or later.

YOUR PHYSICAL FOUNDATION

"The only way to keep your health is to eat what you don't want, drink what you don't like, and do what you'd rather not."
—Mark Twain

Mark's wrong, but you'd be right to question why a section on health is included in a book on personality type. I questioned putting it here.

I'm including it because in my experience, many so-called ENFP struggles are actually rooted in, or exasperated by, poor physical health choices.

Is it normal for an ENFP to change directions every week or is it a result of poor focus and lack of mental clarity caused by a poor diet and lack of physical exercise?

In my experience the tendency to envision alternatives and the drive to explore new possibilities is very much an ENFP trait, but the lack of cognitive control, inability to stay on track, and impulsive changes in direction are primarily a result of broader physical and mental health issues.

Yes, this isn't going to be the most fun chapter but I'll do my best to include some fart jokes.

Your health will ultimately dictate your ability to follow your calling and make an impact.

Even if you have the mental fortitude to run a marathon, without the right training and fitness in the process, you're going to destroy your body. Once your body is destroyed, that mental fortitude you so loved yet abused is likely to suffer.

I've met many ENFPs who have literally willed themselves to keep going and keep going, to push themselves to incredible levels... of burn-out. They find themselves either in the hospital or basically incapacitated for months.

In my personal life I recall warning one ENFP I cared about that she was en route to burnout. All the signs were there. A few months after she dismissed my concern, she wrote me to say she'd moved to the countryside to recover and could barely move, think, or function.

Don't Make Decisions Hungover

For most people the post festive drinking brunch menu features a mix of anxiety, depression, and fuzzy thinking. Some years ago, I recognized something that changed my life: When I made my body physiologically feel something, such as anxiety and depression, from an external input, such as Tequila, my thoughts would change to match the physical reality I was feeling.

Feeling anxious? It couldn't purely be alcohol withdrawal; there must be some deeper reason I should hunt for. This was the starting point of disastrous Saturday mornings. The hangover-induced anxiety would spark negative thoughts and questions about my calling, relationships, or whatever else. Simultaneously, because of this very same hangover, my thinking was too fuzzy to catch my thoughts and redirect my mind.

Welcome the downward spiral.

I eventually made a rule for myself: No thinking about anything big picture or important when you're hungover, exhausted, or sick. Now when I catch my thoughts going this way, I just say to myself, "Dude, you're hungover/exhausted/sick. Your brain is junk. Just hit the sauna and watch some movies. You are not allowed to ponder life today."

I eventually learned that Alcoholics Anonymous has a term, HALT, which means Hungry Angry Lonely Tired. It advises to avoid any of these states as the risk of bad decisions greatly increases. I would advise you to do the same.

Finding The Good

Perhaps you've already been thinking, "But Dan, if making my body feel like shit will trigger bad thoughts, is it possible to trigger good thoughts another way?"

You'd be right. Watch an inspiring movie, go for a run, listen to your favorite songs, or take some cocaine and you'll likely feel more inspired, confident, and excited about the future. I've never done cocaine, myself (and I don't recommend it), but I include it to illustrate that simple physical actions we take can have a dramatic impact on how we feel in the moment and those new feelings will open us up to more positive thoughts on the "big picture" parts of our lives.

This is why a positive routine can be so powerful. Not only does something like running or cold showers have a physiological effect—the physiological effects also change our neurochemistry and that changes how we feel and think. On top of it all, there is the compounding effect of feeling proud of yourself for doing something difficult and sticking to a routine.

Think back to your own experiences. When you've been eating well, exercising, and feeling your best, how do you handle bad news or an unexpected challenge?

Now think about the times you've been run down, hungover, or just at your worse. How quickly can one little thing derail your whole day or even week?

So imagine you've figured out your calling and you're starting to take steps towards creating the life you want and living your calling. Then, all of a sudden, as is inevitable, you hit a roadblock. Your mind starts to go to negative places.

"Maybe I made a mistake."

"Maybe I'm not cut out for this after all."

" I can't do this."

You're now at a crossroads. Down one road is a day, week, or perhaps years spent in a downward spiral of self-doubt and wasted time. This road includes pondering other callings, looking for jobs, and numbing yourself on social media.

The other road includes a kind but firm conversation with that self-doubt. It reminds you that this is normal. Everyone encounters some obstacles but you're committed to going forward because you know you're on the right track. You shrug off the doubtful voices and keep on driving.

In my experience, the exhausted/sick/hungover version of Dan is a lot more likely to drive down self-doubt alley. This is why an investment in physical and mental health is essential to staying on track and creating a life around your calling.

Those who deny their calling turn to addiction and distraction to avoid what they really should be doing.
Steven Pressfield and others have even went so far as to say avoiding our calling and the stress and shame this causes are at the root of most disease.

I don't agree with Steven wholeheartedly. An Uncle of mine who as far as I can tell has lived a life following his passions has had cancer twice. I'm in no place to determine the root causes of disease but I will say this...

> When I'm off track and neglecting my calling, I become a real dick. I'm a worse boyfriend, friend, son, and brother. I'm drawn to news and politics and other toxic areas. I spend much of my time in avoidance mode and when I am with people, I'm in a worse mood.

When I'm focused and excited about a project, such as this book, I am happier, more positive, and less anxious. I am writing this on a Tuesday. Due to travel I have not written since Friday. During those three days, my anxiety levels were rising. In just the last hour since sitting down in this café, I've been feeling better as I proved to myself, " I can still write!" and, " I am not going to leave this book unfinished!"

In my experience there are few if any self-imposed situations as painful as calling purgatory. Knowing you should be doing something more but tiptoeing and dancing back and forth between fear and action... it's an awful feeling.

So I have no doubt that spending too much time in this place, living in a state of avoidance, constantly entertaining fear's ridiculous claims, wreaks havoc on our health and often forms the basis for addictions, illness, and physical pain.

In Summary
▸ Physical Health = Mental Health
▸ Mental Health = Clarity of Thought, Focus, and Persistence
▸ Some People Do Bad Shit When They've Avoiding Good Shit

Oh, and if you're going to be a badass ENFP living your calling and enjoying your dream life, then you're going to need a lot of energy because this is one heck of a party I'm inviting you to.

Why I Care About Health and Finding Your Own Motivation

"Dude, we've made it to the end and we're like 10 years older than most people and the only ones not on drugs"
—Dan to his friend Davide, a few rows from the stage, jumping around like a madman, somewhere around 7 a.m. in the Netherlands, at A State of Trance 1000 with Armin Van Burren.

My motivation around my own health is primarily focused on these outcomes:
▸ Mental Clarity and Focus
▸ Energy
▸ Longevity

Mental clarity and focus because I hate feeling out of control, making poor choices because I'm not thinking clearly, or falling down rabbit holes of time wasting. When I'm cloudy or mentally tired I tend to make bad choices in all areas of my life. Even worse is brain fog, which renders me useless.

Energy because days are long and I want to be able to enjoy as much of them as possible. There were times in my life when I'd be a sloth in the afternoon. As of this writing I'm in my late 30s and it isn't unusual for a day to include a session of beach volleyball, four to five hours of highly focused work, a visit to the gym and sauna, and a night out late into the evening.

Speaking of, I have a friend in his 50s who enjoys similarly packed days. We've discussed the inevitable tradeoff: Late nights and lots of wine today probably mean a little less energy 10 years from now... but (shrug smiley).

This is how I look at longevity: I want to find a balance that enables me to enjoy a glorious lifestyle today while still looking forward to a great future, albeit one with perhaps a few more wrinkles than I'd have if I gave up the wine and went to bed at sunset.

- I want to feel good and trust my thoughts.
- I want to enjoy tonight's party to the very end.
- I want to enjoy the grand party of life until the very end.

You will likely have your own motivations and even different health outcomes. Perhaps these involve grand kids, extreme fitness challenges, or just avoiding some health problems. That said, for most ENFPs, I believe the goals of a clear focused mind, lots of energy, and living for a long time are excellent motivators to treat your mind and body right.

THE CYCLE & WHY IT GETS EASIER

"Because I have a six-pack I can drink all the beer I want. You, it's going to make you fat."

"Well, that doesn't seem particularly fair."

"If you have a certain level of belly fat your body processes carbs differently. When you cut your fat and have more muscles, you're able to handle more carbs without gaining fat."

Travis was talking to me about beer bellies but this sort relationship is happening in many areas of our lives.

The more you exercise and eat well, the clearer your mind becomes and the more mental discipline you develop. This makes it easier to make good choices such as exercising and eating well. Momentum builds and the cycle continues.

The more you play sports, the more friends you make who play sports. These friends invite you to play sports, so you play even more.

None of us have infinite discipline. When you meet someone with an impressive diet or exercise regime it is usually because they unleashed a kangaroo's pouch of discipline over a short period of time and made some big changes. These changes altered their mind, body, and environment to the point where the new way of living became self-sustaining, or at the very least, momentum worked in their favor.

Keto Fast and Furious'd My Brain

When I started the Keto diet in 2018, I was extremely strict. At the same time, I began daily cardio.

These two things combined to give me what could only be described as a supercharged mind. Anyone who has properly done keto knows of this magical clarity and boost in mental energy: It really is profound.

During this time, I also noticed something that I haven't heard discussed anywhere else: I made better choices.

From choosing a book over a video, a salad over cheese, or saying no to that "one last drink," I became intensely aware of what the "good" decision was and I'd almost always choose it. This experience brightened my internal compass and confirmed that I almost always knew what the right thing to do was but that certain mental and physical conditions would previously lead me to "give in" or make poor choices. The more good choices I made the easier it became to make more.

This boost in mental clarity and discipline spilled over into my personal confidence and business. I began to trust myself more and felt like "Future Dan" was someone I could rely on. I took on more ambitious projects, such as hosting my first in-person event, Life Design Fiesta 2018, in Playa Del Carmen, Mexico. Before this, I would have NEVER had the confidence to host a seven-day event where I was training and coaching all day followed by going out with attendees at night.

I share this personal example because at the end of the day, simply changing my diet changed how I thought, how I made decisions, how I felt about myself, and even how I ran my business.

What you choose to do is up to you. I'm not prescribing any specific diet; at the moment I'm not eating keto, but at the end of this section I will include some best practices. But if you find yourself at a low point or in need of a rapid shift in momentum, I have found no quicker way to make a change than diet and exercise. The energy and confidence gained from a new morning run routine, disciplined diet, or working with a trainer will spill over into all areas of your life and start remodeling your self-image in no time.

MY BIGGEST INSIGHTS ON PHYSICAL HEALTH

I never set out to be an expert in all areas of life but I love to learn and am a sponge for information. I decided to include a brief summary of physical health best practices here in case you're a novice and don't want to comb through a dozen of the best books on the topics. At least in Canada and the USA, the government-promoted health information falls somewhere between dated, corrupt, and dangerous.

What Not To Do

▸ Avoid anything processed. Focus on the outside aisles of the supermarket (fruits, veggies, meats, dairy).

▸ For anything packaged, fewer ingredients are almost always better.

▸ Carbs are not your friend.

▸ Fake sugars like high fructose syrup are bad; engineered oils like palm, soy, canola, etc. are even worse.

Make It Easy for Yourself

If you've been on a high carbohydrate diet for a long time it is not easy to suddenly drop carbs. While I have been on and off keto, I found that my time eating keto reset my body and made me "fat adapted" so even when not eating keto I can skip the odd meal without it affecting my mood and I don't crave carbs like I used to.

To be clear, before I did this, I would get extremely moody if I didn't eat and I would lose three to four afternoons a week to the post-lunch energy crash.

Personally, I would try keto for three months, following the book "The Keto Reset Diet," and then find whatever balanced diet works for you. For an ENFP I think this more intense approach is much easier than trying to gradually reduce carbs and fight cravings every day.

If you're interested more in the science, read the book Why We Get Fat by Gary Taubes.

What To Do

- Eat things that are mostly one ingredient and can go bad like fruit, vegetables, and meat.

- Move. Specifically cardio exercise where your heartrate does not go over (180 - (Your Age)) three or more times a week for at least 25 minutes. This pace is where you're breaking a sweat but still able to maintain a conversation.

- Don't hold back! The more you do it the better: Each exercise session creates changes in your brain so you get *more* benefit from future exercise.

- The best kind of exercise includes hand-eye coordination, which activates a part of your mind that has been shown to improve many mental health conditions including ADHD. So something like yoga, boxing, basketball, tennis, or volleyball is ideal.

If you're not in the best shape at the moment, just start by walking. Aside from the health benefits, a good walk without your phone is a wonderful way to clear your head and boost your mood. For more on the science of this, read the book Spark by John J. Ratey.

Intermittent Fasting

This is limiting the times you consume calories. Some people don't consume any calories one day a week. It's more common to eat within an eight-hour window. For example, you would only eat or drink between 12 p.m. and 8 p.m.

I rarely do this intentionally but have seen incredible results in friends who prefer this approach to mental health, weight loss, and longevity over keto. I love to cook, so keto is easy for me, but I have one friend who never cooks and eating out every meal on keto is not easy or enjoyable. So he started intermittent fasting after reading that it's the most effective way to extend your lifespan. One day a week he doesn't consume any calories. Since doing this, his physical transformation has been dramatic. Oh, and this is a guy who used to eat cake three times a day at every meal for years.

My Favorite Books On Physical Health

▸ Why We Get Fat by Gary Taubes
▸ The Keto Reset Diet by Mark Sisson
▸ Spark by John J. Ratey.

Conclusion: Less Is More

When I was younger, I'd always feel busy and stressed. I had no much so to do so of course I couldn't make time for cooking meals or exercising. For the past few years, I've been cooking two to three meals a day and prioritizing exercise and time with friends. I do this because I learned that four hours of focused work with a sharp mind is infinitely more effective than eight cloudy hours. It requires a leap of faith but *I promise if you prioritize your well-being, you will be able to cut your working hours while actually producing and earning more.*

And even if you don't, you'll still be a lot happier and live longer.

ENFP SUPERPOWER

THE ALL-IN GAMBLER

There is plenty of evidence to say the best approach to health involves a consistent and balanced approach.

I choose to ignore this evidence because I'm as likely to be consistent and balanced as I am to get a neck tattoo of Kamala Harris.

ENFPs have the ability to go ALL-IN on something new and often approach it with a tremendous amount of discipline and willpower. This is how I quit drinking alcohol for a year in my mid-20s, did 10-day fasts, or stayed on Keto for over a year.

As you read earlier, in many instances related to diet and exercise, the changes we make change us and make it easier to make better choices in the future. Doing just a two-day water fast wiped out my carb cravings**. Doing keto forever changed my body's relationship to carbs, hunger, and mood swings. Each time you exercise you increase the amount of benefit you get from future sessions.

So taking on a big challenge like running a half-marathon, eating keto for a year, or doing cardio exercise every day for a month might actually be the easier route to long-term change for many ENFPs.

Potential Superpower: To take on big challenges, go all-in, and create lasting change within your body.

Blocks: Take on challenges that you're excited about. You're more likely to run a marathon than you are to "reduce your sugar to 10 grams a day."

Keys To Developing This: Choose something that is going to contribute to lasting changes in your body, habits, and environment.

If you haven't followed through on challenges in the past, be sure to read the upcoming chapter "Making Your Word Count" and go through the process before attempting a new health challenge.

**I do not suggest this water fast approach without consulting a medical professional. Like actually, it can do crazy things with your cortisol levels.

ENFP SUPERPOWER

THE LEARNER

ENFPs love to learn. We love ideas and innovations as much as we love to find solutions to problems. This means we're able to consume information and build our knowledge around a new area very quickly.

This strength, being a quick and enthusiastic learner, is valuable in all areas of life, but I had to put it somewhere, so here it is in our health section.

I was speaking with an ENFP client the other day who discovered he was severely gluten intolerant, so he did a lot of learning on the topic, changed his diet, and began feeling better. While this might seem like the normal, rational thing to do, this same client recounted a story to me of an acquaintance of his who has an autoimmune disease that is often treated successfully with some dietary changes and yet, this acquaintance prefers handfuls of medication, pain, and obesity over doing some reading and making dietary changes.

MANY people cling to the status quo and suffer for years or decades because they're unwilling to invest in learning.

ENFPs on the other hand are keen to develop self-awareness, uncover problems, find solutions, and then take action for a better future.

Potential Superpower: To continuously improve your health, as well as any other area of life you choose, through ongoing learning and experimentation.

Blocks: I joke with friends that if I listen to a podcast that mentions a symptom I have or a benefit I want and suggests a related supplement I'm buying it nine times out of 10. This CAN be good. If someone credible and competent who seems trustworthy suggests a simple product with big potential gains, it would be ridiculous to ignore it.

And... ENFPs who haven't developed their critical thinking abilities can fall victim to all sorts of health fads, BS claims, and downright scams. See the "So Open-Minded Your Brains Fall Out" section on the next pages for more on this.

Keys To Developing This: Start by developing your foundational knowledge in critical thinking as well as whatever area of life you'd like to improve. For example, if you want to improve your health it isn't a bad idea to read, or listen to, a book like "YOU: The Owner's Manual" by Dr. Michael F. Roizen, which provides a high-level overview of how human biology works. If you have no idea how biology, chemistry, or finance work, it is very easy to be manipulated by people with a similar lack of understanding but with much more malice and greed. Just because you add the word quantum to something does not make it brilliant or true.

Then find a few experts in the area you can trust and learn through their books or podcasts. These days you can say just about everything and get a certain amount of agreement, so check for an excessive number of bad reviews or YouTube comments pointing out the person is clueless.

SO OPEN-MINDED YOUR BRAINS FALL OUT

I once spent a Saturday afternoon with a woman who initially impressed me with her knowledge of holistic health. She pointed out how the curve of the waitress's stomach meant she had gluten intolerance. She introduced me to the power of walking barefoot in nature to "ground yourself." She discussed her chocolate healing ceremonies and the radical transformations she has experienced.

She was intelligent and so damn confident I kept an open mind and figured I could learn a thing or two because she did have a really calm and present vibe.

Then:

"The planes are dropping all kinds of chemicals on us"

Oh no. I probe, optimistically, "Do you mean like, they contribute to greenhouse gases?" Please mean this. Please.

"No, like they drop all sorts of chemicals on the cities. That is what those trails are behind the planes."

Oh no. Does this also mean standing barefoot in my garden won't cure my food allergies? Dammit.

Keep It Together

Unfortunately, we live in a world where large organizations and governments have been telling a lot of lies. Everything from the sugar lobby and lies about saturated fat still propagated by many governments, to very questionable data and advisories on the covid vaccines, many people are opening their eyes and doing their own research.

This is great.

Yet something happens once you realize you've been lied to in this area or that. You start to reconsider everything and distrust everything the government or large organizations say.

This is how people make the jump from "factory farming is really bad" to "organic food is better for your baby" to "all vaccines are bad" to "every pilot on earth is part of a vast conspiracy to poison their own friends and family."

There is no simple answer to this problem. I feel grateful to have developed my critical thinking through my education, extensive reading, and life experience. My past work in marketing also trained me to spot lies and manipulation.

How I Find Reliable Information

My approach is to find a few people I can trust and follow them for the long term. This way I can see if they are authentic, honest, and credible.

For example, I started following John Campbell, a nurse practitioner and educator on YouTube in January 2020. At that time, he had 200,000 subscribers and was mostly making videos about biology and health.

I followed John for two years from the start of covid to the end of the pandemic. During this time, I saw him warning of covid and calling for WHO action before any governments or public officials did anything. He was called alarmist.

I saw him being ahead of the news and public advisories every time simply by following the studies and evidence. He never lied, he never mislead, and when he was wrong he would address it and apologize, revising his opinion. Heck, many of his videos are literally him just summarizing peer reviewed studies.

While he was initially a loyal proponent of government recommendations and a big advocate of vaccines, masks, and lockdowns, his opinions started to change, as many people's did, after governments refused to change as new evidence came out. I saw him change his opinions in a thoughtful and rational way as the evidence changed. For example, in early 2022 Denmark was discouraging its citizens from wearing masks and stopped promoting the vaccine, encouraging people to go back to enjoying life. At this same time the government in my homeland Canada was still scaring the pants off, and masks on, my parents.

The Scandinavian countries changed their views as the evidence changed as did John Campbell and for doing so, he was labeled right wing and a conspiracy theorist.

This kind and thoughtful man I'd followed for two years is neither. Trusting him got me through the pandemic in style as I was able to plan ahead and ultimately spent most of the pandemic in villas in Spain and Portugal. In all that time he simply presented the latest stats and studies and, as is one of his taglines, "followed the evidence."

John is one of my foundational pillars of knowledge around public health. I trust him and so I can also spot the lies when news organizations or journalists looking for clicks write an attack piece of him.

I have people like John in different areas of life, from health and fitness to psychology to business. Unfortunately, these days, many "journalists" and content producers are either biased, corrupt, or just not very bright, but there are still credible, thoughtful, and trustworthy people out there and finding and following them is how I protect myself.

Tip #1 — One way to spot people who don't know what they're talking about is to investigate their advice or opinions in areas you are familiar with. If they appear to be ideological, biased, or just plain wrong in an area you know well, assume they are also this way in all the areas you aren't familiar with.

Tip #2 — See if someone can converse on a topic for more than a few minutes and move beyond talking points. One reason I trust John is his daily videos are typically around 30 minutes with few edits.

Ideologically motivated people, and those who don't know the facts, tend to hide behind short segments or highly produced content that can be heavily edited.

STRATEGIES FOR FOLLOWING THROUGH

Use People

ENFPs are most accountable when we are accountable to other people. Every time I've stuck with an exercise practice I didn't intrinsically enjoy—lifting weights in my case—it has been because of a personal trainer or workout partner. Every single time.

If there is something you want to do more of, the easiest way is to make friends who do that thing. It sounds simple and it is.

Make It Fun

Remember Aaron? He was my client from Germany who made a living running a movement studio in Hong Kong teaching people how to do flips, jump off walls, that kind of stuff. I asked him how he was able to stay so disciplined with it, perhaps assuming it had something to do with his German heritage, and he told me he wasn't disciplined at all. He could never go lift weights on a regular basis. He did this, and stuck with it, because each day was totally new and something fun he looked forward to.

Make It Easy & Plan for Weakness

My flight landed in Prague at 1 a.m. It had been a long day, starting around 8 a.m. and mostly spent on my feet or intensely working. I arrived home starving but assuming my fridge would be empty, planning to go to bed hungry. Now that I was back in Prague, I would be eating strictly keto for the summer. Then I saw the note:

> "Welcome Home! There is something for you in the fridge"
> —Svet

The kindness of my assistant warmed my heart and past me would have been over the moon to see a full pizza waiting for me in the fridge.

Svet could not have known I was starting keto and that facing down a full pizza, 8 hours after my last meal and exhausted,was a temptation landmine.

I declared, "I'm just going to eat the cheese and toppings!" and to the applause of millions, I actually stuck to this. No crust, no carbs.

The next day I went out with a few different friends and stuck with my diet. Damn, I was proud of myself. Momentum was really building.

The next afternoon I checked the freezer for anything to throw out. Oh no. No.

NOOOOOOOOOOO.

Guests staying at my apartment while I was away had left three of four mini Häagen-Dazs ice cream tubs. At any other point in life, this would have been a welcome gift but today... today...

"Well, there is no way I can throw these out and also, there is no way I can't eat them. It's Häagen-Dazs. Better to eat them all at once so I can get it over with."

And so I did. After surviving the pizza and the next day out, I finally stepped on a landmine I couldn't avoid.

We all have a limited reserve of cognitive energy. Many factors influence how much or little we have but there is always a limit. When an action is clear and there is no choice—such as someone like myself, deathly allergic to peanuts, not eating peanuts—no cognitive energy is wasted. I have no internal debate about whether or not I should have "just a little" peanut butter. The same is true when you set strict rules for yourself about what you do and do not eat. Rules set in stone free up your cognitive energy.

Do not punish yourself with unnecessary temptation. Set strict rules and keep your environment free of temptations. Once you begin debating if you should finish off that Häagen-Dazs or bag of chips friends left behind, you've already lost the battle. Even if you land on the right side, you'll have wasted crucial cognitive energy you could have spent elsewhere.

So yes, this means when I am eating keto I don't have ANY carbs in the house and I never do cheat days. It just isn't worth it.

Whether we are talking about my carb addiction, eating and health, electronics and social media, or anything else, the best way to avoid addictions and build good habits is to set firm rules AND set up your environment for success. Make it easy for yourself. Eliminate temptation and have alternatives on hand.

If you're breaking a social media addiction, what could you do to meet those same needs? Maybe it's reading an interesting book for mindless distraction, calling a friend for social contact, or heading to the beach to see half-naked strangers.

Being a Source of Inspiration

At weddings people always ask about the lack of cake on my plate and beer in my mug. So I explain. Perhaps I mention the benefits I've experienced and dispel the myths around keto, such as that you only eat meat or can't drink alcohol. In the end, you can be sure If I am invited to a wedding at least 3 people will leave that wedding committed to ditching the carbs.

I've found that helping others with their health is reenergizing and recommits me. Not wanting to be a hypocrite, I can't rave about keto for an hour than eat a pizza right? Not only does it feel great to help others, and I've seen the results in my friends, it makes it easier for me to stick with my commitments.

ENFPs love to inspire others and create change and will enjoy huge benefits when they are inspiring others to be their best as well.

MAKE YOUR WORD COUNT

"Until you're ready to look foolish, you'll never have the possibility of being great."
—Cher

I've never met anyone so capable of enthusiasm for an event in the future than my younger self. I was an idea generator ready to say yes at every opportunity with such confidence nothing could stand in my way.
This confidence and enthusiasm often came before the realization of what it would feel like, in those future moments, as I trudged through the actual work.

This impulsive enthusiasm, combined with my tendency to think out loud and share ideas before I've really considered all the aspects, lead to a brief period where I didn't always trust myself to do what I said and an even briefer period where my word meant essentially nothing, even to myself.

If you've been a bit slippery with your word lately and would like some tips for rebuilding your trust in yourself this section is for you. When you make your word matter you'll sense a new respect from others, learn to trust yourself on a deeper level, and discover it's much easier to finish things.

Your Word Must Matter

For anything I've shared in this book to matter your own word must matter. Whether it is being a great friend or partner, adopting a healthier way of living, or going all in pursuing your dreams: **Your word has to matter. You must be able to trust yourself.**

I believe your subconscious is always watching your behavior and forming a belief system about who you are based on how you act. If you lie you become a liar, not only to others, but to yourself. How likely are you to "wake up at 7 a.m. every day!" or "give up carbs!" if your own image of yourself is that of a liar?

Not very.

If you lie and deceive in one area of your life you will lie and deceive in all of them and that ultimately means not even being able to trust yourself. That's bad.

Fortunately, there is hope...lots of it. If you needed any more motivation, here are a few more reasons to make your word count.

You'll Live, and Sleep, Better

Ever notice how many TV shows and Movies revolve around lies? That romantic comedy could have been a 30 second commercial if he just told her how he felt. That family drama could have been a YouTube video if everyone just spoke the truth and kept their word. Lies create drama and drama is bad for business.

> Instead of getting my need for excitement met from upsetting interpersonal drama or a stressful work situation, I'd much rather take a trip, go for a hike, or try something new.

People Will Present More Opportunities

When you're someone that can be trusted you'll suddenly find yourself with a wealth of new opportunities in all areas of life. Not only will people trust you, they'll admire you because there aren't that many people whose word means anything these days. This feels nice.

You'll Become Superhuman

At the peak of my word being unbreakable I was able to simply declare a change, such as quitting alcohol for a year, or waking up at 6 a.m. every day, and it would happen. I could create a schedule, broken down into specific work and break times, and I'd follow it simply because I promised to do so.

How To Make It Happen

I have built, destroyed, and rebuilt my word multiple times in my life. I know, without a doubt, you can do the same if you commit and follow this process.

Baby steps. This is the only way to do it. *Avoid all your ENFP tendencies to go all in with some massive declaration about how you'll never lie again.*

Seriously.

Step One: Stop Making Unnecessary Promises

Adjust your language to say "try" instead of "will"; use "aiming for" instead of "it will be done on".

Yes, I know who Yoda is. I know the school of thought that says make everything a must, but that only works once your word means something: If that isn't currently the case you need to go back to square one to get it there.

Also, stop saying yes to anything you don't want to do. You can apply the "Hell YES or Hell NO" approach. If you aren't really excited about something, say NO. If you feel rude just tell the other person "I'm doing an experiment where I'm not committing to anything I can't be 100% sure I'll be able to do". If this is really hard for you, I suggest spending 2 days where you force yourself to say no to EVERYTHING anyone else proposes to get over this discomfort.

Step Two: Build The Muscle

Now that you stopped committing to things you weren't ever going to do, it is time to make your word matter one thing at a time.

Oh, and by the way, I'm granting you a 100% clean slate starting NOW. I hereby absolve you of all past misuse of your word. From this moment forward, you are 0 of 0 for your word.

Do it with me right now. Say to yourself *"Now, I am going to snap my fingers."*

Now, *snap your fingers.*

AMAZING. You just made your word count. You're now 1 for 1, you have a 100% record of staying true to your word.

Now, keep this up. As silly as it sounds, start by stating things you know you will clearly do, right before doing them. "I'm going to drink a glass of water" with the glass in your hand, "I'm going to go for a walk" with your shoes on.

Gradually expand this. *Do not make bold commitments or promise daily activities like "I'm going to do yoga every day".* At least not at this stage, but perhaps not at any stage. *You'll have better luck maintaining your word if you make declarations on a daily or weekly basis.*

If you follow these instructions you will be blown away at how quickly your word comes to mean something, your self image shifts, and you develop the ability to direct your behavior by simply saying so.

You Don't Need To Be Perfect

I know it's going to be tempting to keep that percentage at 100 right? It is OK if you don't, in fact, it's totally normal.

Elon Musk, like many visionaries, is rather famous for declaring many deadlines he never meets. We'll have this product out next month! Two years later it is released.

At times it's OK to make bold declarations, even if you miss them, because the declaration can create forward momentum and get you there faster than if you set a realistic goal. Heck, in many cases, a realistic goal is going to be so "meh" you won't even bother getting started in the first place.

> Just choose your words carefully. Perhaps say "I'm striving for" or " I want to have it ready for" instead of " I absolutely promise it will be ready on". Never, ever, make a promise you're not 100% committed to making happen.

What I won't do is tell little, or big, lies just to make my life easier. If I'm late to a meeting I will just apologize for being late without an explanation rather than include a little lie about this or that.

If you like to gamify things, you could always do something where you count how often you follow through on your word up to 10, and after that if you miss something, allow yourself a reset to begin over. See how many times you can get to 10 in a month.

Avoid Public Emotional Statements

Us ENFPs love to make big declarations. This is the #1 reason I get invited to parties. *It is also the #1 reason I don't get invited to dinner parties.*

I love public declarations of my goals as a form of accountability but I don't think you should do this until you're 100% ready to follow through. Just as you might need to rebuild the trust in your word with yourself, you may also need to rebuild it with other people. So start with things like calling when you said you would and gradually improve from there.

Just Say It, Especially When It's Hard

Sometimes telling the truth is hard. What if you have a date with someone and during the date you feel good, but later you don't feel like seeing the person again? You stare at your phone, unable to type the words that are so clear in your head: *I just don't really like you.*

A member of your family asks why you haven't called recently. You can't bring yourself to tell them *I just didn't want to talk to you.*

I'm not going to advocate radical honesty here but I'll encourage you to:

1) Say something!
2) Tell the truth!

You don't have to tell him he had the fashion sense of garden gnome, " I had a nice time, but I don't want to go out again" or "You're a xyz person, but I'm just not feeling it romantically" will do just fine. Send it and be done. You can tell that family member " I was in a bit of a weird headspace and just didn't feel like talking."

I once got this gem of a text from a fellow ENFP who was on vacation in Spain when I asked for another date:

> "Hey Dan, unfortunately I've a lot I want to do before I leave and I'll prioritize those. It has been nice to live this little adventure with you though. Take care."

Hey, gotta respect her honesty!

Accept The Pain

Whenever I go on the Keto diet I need to remind myself of two things to make it work:

1) I'm going to spend a lot more money on food, but the return on investment in focus and energy is worth it 10x.

2) Something I adapted from Coco Chanel: "Nothing tastes as good as keto feels."

Sometimes being on keto sucks, but the long term benefits to my life are always worth it. It is the same thing with telling the truth. In the short term lying is easy. It saves you time and effort and sometimes avoids uncomfortable situations.

It's the equivalent of a slice of pizza or kebab on the way home. "What's the harm" many people would say. Well for me, that one slice of pizza is going to turn into dozens over the month because I know that if I have an easy option available to me I am not going to put in the effort to cook a proper dinner. When you remove lying you'll be forced to cook that healthy dinner and I promise you the rewards will be vast.

> You have to start with the truth. The truth is the only way that we can get anywhere. Because any decision-making that is based upon lies or ignorance can't lead to a good conclusion.
> —Julian Assange

PART VI

ENFPS AT WORK

I wish for you to spend your days challenged, excited, and forever growing while contributing to others as a force for good in whatever area you're passionate about.

Oh, and at least 4 weeks of vacation per year. *At least!*

THE CANADIAN IN SPAIN

"Love and work are the cornerstones of our humanness"
—Sigmund Freud

I must confess: I love to work.

My love defies some misinformed yet commonly shared stereotypes about ENFPs. My Calling is one of the best parts of my life. I love what I do and it serves a purpose. I like the people I work with and I genuinely look forward to Monday mornings.

I'm sure you've heard the ol' "Americans live to work, Europeans work to live." In the past, I've used this adage as an example of how European life is more relaxed, healthy, and balanced than in the U.S. and my native Canada.

Now I have more nuanced views.

How we spend the majority of our time is incredibly important. Sure, we North Americans live to work. But we do it because, often, the work feels significant and we don't get that much joy from sipping a tiny cappuccino for three hours. I do enjoy sitting at a cafe for hours, but only if, like this very moment, I'm writing.

I don't want to sit around doing nothing. I literally *can't*. I have important work to do!

To be fair, I think Americans work too many hours and take too few vacations, not only from a moral or values perspective, but from a simple effectiveness one. Your ROI on time and energy greatly diminishes after about seven hours of work per day.

Yet there is a reason retired, often lower-income, Brits retire to Spain while the intelligent and ambitious young Spanish move to the UK. We need forward momentum in our lives to be happy, and one of the primary ways we get that is by pursuing a calling, including creative and entrepreneurial pursuits that ultimately support our freedom.

I've been on the other side, mind you. I've spent a few years with an entirely passive income. I'm currently running a business where I could only work 10 hours a week if I chose, or even less. I've chosen to live by the beach for significant periods of my life. And you know what...

> Not once have I found myself thinking "Wow, if I could just lie here on the beach all day every day, I'd be happy."

If you find yourself thinking "Piss off Dan, I want the beach life," I can immediately tell you one thing: Your current job does not meet the perfect ENFP Calling criteria.

If you're pushing papers in a hamster wheel, *of course* you'd crave the beach. If you're working 50 hours a week without a clue what your work actually accomplishes, or taking orders from a boss you don't respect, *of course* you're going to crave freedom and a lack of responsibility. But idleness is not your real destination—it's a vacation en route.

ENFPs have a lot of energy. Our intuition means we're future-oriented. We are creators, and we are movers and shakers. We need something creative to apply ourselves to in order to continually grow and learn new things—otherwise, we go insane with boredom.

So how do you pick a career?

I'm glad you asked, because it's extremely important.

Getting your vocation right, whether you're working for someone else or planting your own flag, is critical for your happiness. Settling or taking someone else's suggestions doesn't work. If you're browsing Help Wanted ads or Googling college degrees instead of sitting down and thinking through what you actually want, you've already lost the battle.

I didn't open an internet browser and search "What kind of business can I do?" and you shouldn't either. If you're looking for inspiration, you're better off avoiding click bait articles and mass produced "content" and reading autobiographies, talking to other passionate people, and bouncing ideas around than staring dead-eyed at a soulless search engine. Learn the fundamentals of business and value creation, find an idea that fuels your fire, take charge, and design the business and life you want.

In the following chapters I'm going to lay out the essential elements of a fulfilling vocation for any ENFP. I've reluctantly included a list of well-matched careers, but if you only focus on that and not the other elements here, you're entirely missing the point. You're letting the outside world present you with a menu.

What I'm suggesting is that you design your perfect meal and then call the chef over.

Bon appetit.

CAREER OR CALLING?

Career: An occupation undertaken for a significant period of a person's life and with opportunities for progress.
Calling: A strong urge towards a particular way of life or career; a vocation.

 I hope you don't feel mislead, but we aren't actually going to talk about your career here. I get it, you have bills to pay, expectations to live up to, dreams to kill off. Picking a career the old fashioned way is an excellent way to achieve all these things.

The reason you should stop thinking in terms of careers and start thinking in terms of calling is right there in the definition of career: "undertaken for a significant period of a person's life."

Significant period is an understatement. I have spent a significant period of my life on airplanes, playing Starcraft, and eating tacos. Many people will spend the **majority** of their waking life doing something related to their career.

If you refuse to be proactive and design your life, that significant period for many people ends up being about half your waking hours. Here I am including things like a commute and the headspace taken on weekends. It isn't really any better if you work at home or have a job that you don't think about during off hours. This just means you don't have any office social life or relationships or that you're not excited by your work.

If you're going to be spending a significant amount of your life doing something, perhaps up to 50% of your waking hours, doesn't it make sense to pursue your calling?

> If you're an ENFP driven to learn and improve, always wanting to grow, doesn't it make sense to focus your growth around your calling so that one day you can be one of the best in the world?

What Is the ENFP Calling?

Your calling, should you choose to accept it, is to positively impact the lives of those around you. To bring light to darkness and illuminate possibilities others have missed. To turn frowns into smiles, doubts into dreams, reasons to quit into reasons to continue. Your calling is to be the person that brings life to a room, the person who is missed when you leave and whose presence and impact will never be forgotten.

Oh, that's all Dan? Phew. I was worried you were going to say I needed to learn Excel.

Actually, there's more. While bringing light to darkness is an excellent starting point, for some ENFPs, your calling may go even further. You'll use your wisdom and intuition to spot what isn't working in you, in others, in a company, or in society as a whole, and to offer new possibilities for how we can all live.

And it will be easier than you think. For us ENFPs, it is always easier to go big and follow our strengths. When we do, we harness a tremendous potential that exists in each of us.

ENFPs Are Special

Just recently, in the midst of writing this very book, I created The ENFP Reboot: A personal challenge to publish a video daily for 30 days. If you're so inclined, you can watch the series on the books resource page: www.DreamsAroundTheWorld.com/Calling

Before I committed to the challenge, I failed to publish even ONE video each month for the past few months. My YouTube channel and podcast were a disappointing mess. I was caught up in the past, angry with a dishonest video editor who let me down, and had lost all enthusiasm for both creating and coaching.

Then, BOOM. Doing something that was arguably 30 times harder than publishing one video a month was easier and more enjoyable.

ENFP MATH
Publish 1 Video = Hard
Publish 31 Videos = Easy

OK, so let's assume you're on board with the ambitious calling I've laid out above. If you're the practical type, you're thinking, "Yeah, this is great and all, I'm feeling inspired, but, like, can you give me a job title?"

Yes and no. I promise to get into some specific businesses, services, and even jobs that can be great for ENFPs, but if you jump right to that list you'll be doing yourself and your ability to create your own life a great disservice.

I said your calling is "to positively impact the lives of those around you. To bring light to darkness and illuminate possibilities others have missed. To turn frowns to smiles, pessimists to optimists, reasons to quit to reasons to continue. Your calling is to be the person who brings life to a room, the person who is missed when you leave, and whose presence and impact will never be forgotten."

Where and how you apply this, in terms of what industry and what skills you use...that's up to you. Your calling is about how you approach your work and how you impact the people you give value to.

I'm writing this section from a very laptop-friendly cake shop in Valencia, Spain. The comfy chairs, great tables, friendly staff, and wonderful coffee...the owner of this shop has given me the gift of working on my calling today whether or not she knows it.

Through my ENFP Unleashed Coaching Program and Community, I have met hundreds of ENFPs living their calling in a range of countries, industries, and services.

Aaron is a German ENFP who was living in Hong Kong. He is one of those guys who can jump off walls and do backflips for days. He used his love of variety and passion for movement to inspire his students to become more active, healthy, and flexible through his, well, movement school.

Marina, discussed in more detail later, is a Ukrainian American living in Prague. Her day job is curing cancer but her passion is the life-changing potential of yoga. She helps people, including me, be at their best through her studio in Prague, Yoga & Rest.

ENFPs do gravitate towards coaching, teaching, and wellbeing service businesses, but that is not our calling. I have met ENFP Doctors, Lawyers, Realtors, Accountants, Financial Advisers, and Teachers who live out their calling every day by HOW they work and the impact they have on their clients.

I worked as a freelance copywriter for a few years, funding my first few years of travel as I lived in Costa Rica, New York, Germany, Italy, and Spain. I used my ENFP wiring to see the best in my clients, capture their talents and unique voice, and help them feel confident about their services.

> "Find a subject you care about and which you in your heart feel others should care about. It is this genuine caring, and not your games with language, which will be the most compelling and seductive element in your style."
> Kurt Vonnegut

Let's just be clear: I am not advocating that all ENFPs run out and get a job. As I will passionately explore in the chapter on entrepreneurship, I think ENFPs move to the beat of their own drum and many of us will eventually be happiest working for ourselves or within a partnership. Still, there are many times when the right job can be extremely beneficial and there are some fields that only really work within a larger organization.

> At the same time, if you decide to be the master of your own destiny you still need to design your own business and your role within it to suit your personality so almost everything we're going to cover here applies to working for yourself, with others, or for others.

What Matters

Spoiler alert: You need to care… and caring isn't enough.

ENFPs tend to have higher than average IQs, meaning we learn and adapt quickly. Throw in a dash of people pleasing and we can do pretty well in just about anything—at least for a year or two. Even without any real passion for the topic at hand, many ENFPs are able to excel in more technical jobs based on this intelligence and adaptability alone.

I remember speaking to a client of mine—you remember Marina—about how she keeps getting promoted. Despite owning a Yoga studio on the side, she can't help but do well in her main career as a team lead at a biotech company. She keeps getting moved up and handed more responsibility.

She very candidly disclosed to me, "We are literally curing cancer… and I really don't care. I don't feel any connection with it." By coincidence, earlier that day I was speaking to Ashwina, a hair colorist in Los Angeles with a degree in computer science.

So here we have a computer scientist who prefers to color hair, and a successful manager who prefers to teach yoga.

What's happening here? Is it entitled millennials showing a truly offensive lack of responsibility? A dismissal of capitalism and crazy working hours?

Neither. Both are type A women who consistently impress me with their work ethic and focus. They're rockstars with plenty of financial ambition. And they aren't even millennials.

They confirmed a theory I've had for years:

> ENFPs only care when we experience an actual human connection in, and through, our work.

I guarantee that an ENFP serving meals face-to-face will feel more fulfillment than one working for an organization eliminating global poverty if the latter is working behind spreadsheets on the other side of the world from the people she is helping. Our emotional experience is dictated by what we *actually* experience and feel *on a regular basis*.

I've experienced this firsthand. I've had weeks where I wasn't speaking with clients, during which I would feel more satisfaction from giving a waiter a bit of business advice in a casual conversation than I'd feel from filming half a dozen videos for YouTube. Intellectually, I know that right now there are 100-200 people somewhere in the world watching a video of mine. Many of them may be touched or even changed by that video. But like a wife eying her husband's beer belly, it ain't doing anything for me.

I've done my best to adjust my own business to be as satisfying as it can while still be location independent. I don't offer purely automated video courses and I love hosting intimate group coaching calls and multiday in-person events.

> I know I could make more money if I just automated everything but then I wouldn't feel anything, and I'd lose my gas. It isn't just about us having the why—it is about us feeling the why.

Not to mention I know my fellow ENFPs; you are going to get 100 times better results working with me if there is a human element and a real connection.

I believe this is one of the many reasons for the massive corporate exodus that happened during the pandemic. Working from home, deprived of office flirting, post-work cocktails, and an enjoyable and enriching podcast commute, people are faced with the boring reality of their work.

It's like shitty American food. Take away the buckets of sauce, extra sugar, and all the other coverups, and you're left with some pretty awful core ingredients.

When you're looking for a job, the *day-to-day* experience of what you'll be doing is *infinitely* more important than the company's "mission."

Working For The Devil

Just because the day-to-day is more important than the mission does *not* mean the mission is irrelevant. The butter might be more important in your dish than the salt, but you need both.

If you're working for a company that has a negative impact on the world, you'll eventually go a little bonkers—even if you enjoy the work. Perhaps especially if you do. it's like, "Wait, so the more iPhones I sell, the more Uighurs get imprisoned. Hmmm."

But when I stop and think about the positive impact my work has, it does give me a nice feeling.

We can now start to build a list here:
1. The day-to-day of the job.
2. The company's purpose.

That's not a mistake. This is my book and I can go in whatever order I want.

There's something more important than the company's purpose: your immediate manager or leader. This is not just my theory—it's been proven by Gallup research and discussed at length by experts like Marcus Buckingham in *First, Break All the Rules*.

It's also common sense. If you're at a great company but your boss is a moron, you're not going to be happy. If you're at a so-so company but admire and respect your boss and you do great work together, you'll probably be fairly happy.

1. The day-to-day of the job.
2. Your immediate manager or leader.
3. The company's purpose.

The list above might help explain why what seemed like a perfect job on paper turned out to be so disagreeable. It may also give you some ideas for interview questions.

WHAT, WHO, AND HOW

"It's not 'What do I want to do?', it's 'What kind of life do
I want to have?—Arianna Huffington

You've probably been expecting a whole section, or at the very least,
a chapter, dedicated to finding your why. After all, "Why" is a certain
famous ENFP's favorite word; He wrote a whole book about it.

Sorry but you're all out of luck. Telling an ENFP they need to know
why they're doing something, that they need to believe in whatever
they're doing, is more of a waste of paper than those 500 page bills in
congress no one ever reads.

You already know this. You've known this since primary school
when you asked the teacher why you need to follow stupid rules. You've
known since secondary school when you questioned your French/
Spanish/German teacher's insistence that you memorize the gender of
objects before you could even order a juice. Heck, perhaps you even
questioned the absurdity of assigning gender to inanimate objects...or
if you're a recent graduate, perhaps you questioned why the objects ar-
en't allowed to choose their own genders in France.

"How does knowing the gender of the juice help me if I don't know
how to ask for it?!"

"Dan, just memorize the list".

Thank god for Altavista Translate...passed that French class with a
beautiful 51% and never looked back.

What Drives Us ENFPs?

For ENFPs, our gasoline is our Why. We need it to run or this car isn't
going anywhere.

Oh right, Elon. Okay, well, old cars didn't run without gasoline. Just
pretend it's 2002, okay? Spiderman, the first of many, had just opened
#1 in theaters, Nickelback was topping the charts, and physicians

everywhere were advising patients to load up on the carbs if they wanted to be healthy.

OK, so without gas a car doesn't run. And when you get into the inner workings of an engine, the more gas a car can burn in a moment, the more power and speed it has. This is our Why. Generally, the more the better, assuming you can actually experience and feel your contribution to your Why.

If you can't experience your Why, if you can't really feel it, it almost doesn't matter.

More on that later.

Beyond Why

There are 3 other elements that actually determine our success at work, whether working for ourselves or something else. This is where I'm going to focus. Those other elements are the What, How, and Who.

The **What** is like a car's tires.

The **How** is the road conditions.

The **Who** is like your best friend who just hopped the fence of prison and is waiting for his getaway driver (you) to get there before they notice she tunneled out.

If your tires—the What—are in fine working order, then all that gasoline—your Why—can be directly applied to the ground and give you forward momentum.

If the road and weather conditions are great, you'll have no problem staying on course and reaching your destination in time.

And that friend of yours waiting in a ditch for her ride to Mexico, well, she's the real thing that keeps you going. You're an ENFP and even if everything else falls apart, you're going to do whatever it takes to be there for your tribe, your family.

So you have your gasoline, your new tires, sunny days and smooth roads, and your friend's freedom keeping you accountable.

Odds of success = 100%.

But what if we remove any one of these elements?

> What happens if your tires (your What) are flat? What
> happens if the road conditions (your How) are horrible?
> Or what if it turns out your friend really did know about
> those 6kg of cocaine in her bag... and she didn't even offer
> to cut you in on the profits? That's what we are going to
> explore in this chapter.

It goes without saying that we're aiming for you to find a calling with all 4 elements perfectly aligned, but that might not be the case now and it might also take some years to get there. I am my own boss and yet, it has still been a journey to get my Why, What, How, and Who in alignment. At times I've even been there only to slide back or lose an element or two. Sometimes we must tackle a What or How we aren't suited for to get over a hurdle or move things forward.

For example, I'm quite sure I am going to end up taking on some of the editing and publishing functions of this book. Not ideal, but it is a one-time sacrifice I'm willing to make that will hopefully move me forward and give me time to find the perfect partners for my next book.

You might find it useful to take these four areas and use them to evaluate your business or job each month with the aim of reaching the promised land in each of the four. Just remember that you might only make little bits of progress on each one at a time and that's OK.

Let's start with some definitions and then look at the most common scenarios I've seen in my coaching work.

Why: Your fuel. The ultimate purpose behind what you are doing. The best Why is linked to something larger than yourself that can even continue beyond your lifetime.

What: The topic and deliverable of what you're doing. For example, you teach IT skills, you present environmental research, you help people invest, you fight fires.

The What is your path to fulfill your Why. For example, if your Why is to stop losses from fire, your What could be going into burning buildings with a hose, but it could also be teaching fire prevention or lobbying governments for tougher regulations.

How: How is the details of how you execute your What. For example, say you decide on preventing fires via education... how could you approach this? There are really dozens of options, from writing to podcasting to online videos, speaking in schools, or giving demonstrations on street corners. It is essential to find the How most aligned with your natural preferences.

Who: Who describes the people you work with, including business partners, colleagues, employees, and clients.

The Ideal We're Striving For

Why - Fuels you in the deepest sense. Thinking about the change you'll affect gives you goosebumps.

What - You're intensely fascinated by the topic(s) you engage with and the industry you work in.

How - You get results by spending the majority of your time working in your strengths and are keenly rewarded for using your Ne (Extraverted Intuition). It isn't unusual for you to end the day with more energy than you started with.

Who - The people you work with are smart, inspiring, and open-minded. They focus on outcomes over methods and give you room to operate your own way. They rarely, if ever, utter the phrase "because those are the rules."

When You're Missing Some Pieces

Scenario One: The Empty Tank

Have: What, How, Who
Don't Have: Why

Outcome: You're probably young or started this career when you were and have just stuck with it. You got into it before you developed your Fi and started to think about the larger impact you want to have on the world.

You're going be able to keep going and have a moderate level of career success but it's likely you'll feel like your tanks are empty a lot more often than you should. That drive, zest, and crazy high levels of energy so many ENFPs have... well, you ain't going to have them.

Action: Can you make some changes and bring your personality into your career? Is it possible to find an inspiring Why within your industry? I'm not talking some fluffy "Well, by selling industrial cleaning supplies, I'm able to keep schools clean and that helps kids learn and so basically I'm educating the future generation" bullshit Why. I'm talking about something you can really feel on a day to day basis. If not, and if feeling happy, energized, and full of life is important to you, you might want to consider a change.

Scenario Two: Burnout

Have: Why, Who, Possibly What
Don't Have: How, Possibly What

Outcome: Imagine you have all the fuel in the world and an intense motivation to reach your destination but your tires are flat and old and the road conditions are horrible.

What's going to happen?

A crash like you've never seen before. That is why I call this combination the ENFP Burnout Recipe. We'll force ourselves to do work we don't enjoy, in a way that isn't aligned with our functions, because we believe in the Why and don't want to disappoint our Who. (Also, burnout is a car thing.)

Action: You've got to change the How or you will burn out. There is a strong chance you're relying on your above average intelligence combined with your desire to please. This can keep you going for a short time, like the chase scene in a movie, but eventually you're going to burn out.

It might be uncomfortable, but you must have an open and honest conversation with whoever you work with. It is infinitely better to avert course before a burnout than after… once the burnout happens you are in for at least a year of recovery and will have done permanent damage to your body and career.

One sign you're on the verge of a burnout? The belief that your work is too important and it would be impossible to take even a few days off.

Scenario Three: It's All For Them!

Have: Who

Don't Have: Why, What, How

Outcome: This is the scenario so many people could suddenly see clearly during the Covid pandemic. Working remotely essentially robbed them of the Who element since they would no longer meet colleagues in person. Stripped of their colleagues, community, and cocktails—left only with their "work"—tens of thousands of people realized how pointless, boring, and frustrating their "work" really was.

Action: These sort of jobs suck, but *might* be okay to hang onto for a bit if they allow you to gain more freedom and pursue something bigger.

Scenario Four: I Hate These People

Have: Why, What, How

Don't Have: Who

Outcome: This is most common for ENFP entrepreneurs and some-times those with very autonomous remote jobs. In these scenarios, we are often alone and missing the inspiration and synergy ENFPs can get from working with others.

It can also happen when a job is perfect for you but your immediate manager or team are an awful fit.

Action: If you're working for yourself or relatively autonomously, look for opportunities to increase your interactions. Do not hire people because you're lonely or bring on a business partner that doesn't com-plement you. Instead, look for smaller opportunities such as collabora-tions or partnerships in specific areas of your business.

Other Scenarios

There are of course many other possible combinations, and perhaps you've been able to identify the scenario you're in. If you have two or few-er "haves," you likely already know what you're doing isn't right for you.

Next Steps

If you're deciding what to do next in terms of your calling, consider ALL four elements when choosing. Interview people doing what you want to do and find out what their day-to-day looks like.

> Interview people at the top of the game and ask yourself:
> "If I achieved great success, made it to this level, and had
> this person's life, would I be happy?"

If you're already traveling down your path, use these four areas to evalu-ate your current work and decide what needs to change to bring it into full alignment with your personality.

CALLINGS FOR ENFPS

"Give a man a fish and you feed him for a day, teach a man
to fish and you feed him for a lifetime."—Lao Tzu

This quote hits very close to home for me. I grew up in a fishing village in Canada. My Dad was a vice president at one of the biggest seafood companies in Canada. We had unlimited access to fresh salmon and any other seafood one's heart desired.

I was also severely allergic to seafood until my 20s. There's no lesson here; I just think it's a rather funny personal fact I wanted to share.

As for teaching a man to fish, it turns out it really isn't so simple these days. The salmon run only happens for a short time each year and it's heavily regulated by the government. When and how one can fish is dictated by the Canadian Fisheries department and it changes every year.

So for some, what could be a simple fulfilling dream job living on the water becomes an exercise in bureaucracy, politics, and market manipulation.

This echoes my experience with many professions: From teaching to law, marketing to manufacturing...times are changing.

In my teens and 20s, I adored advertising and read the books of every famous ad man. I loved the challenge and creativity. I even started my own advertising agency at one point.

In 2012 I was working as a freelance copywriter while spending the summer in Manhattan. One day I was walking down East 14th and noticed this woman matching my pace. You know how it is: You both just happen to walk at about the same pace and catch the same red lights while pretending not to notice what's happening. The woman is trying to access the odds you're a serial killer and you're desperately trying to project a *I'm not a serial killer, I really live in this direction too!* vibe.

This was 2012 and it was still acceptable to talk to strangers so I do eventually say hi and we begin to chat. This was pleasant because walking and talking was much easier than thinking about not looking like a serial killer. As the conversation progressed she mentions her job at Ogilvy advertising agency. Clearly impressed, I tell her I'd read David Ogilvy's book and creating ads for Ogilvy is one of my dreams. She asks about what I'm doing, which at the moment was freelance copywriting while traveling the world, having recently moved to Manhattan from Costa Rica.

"Trust me, you're living the dream all of us have. The advertising world isn't the creative fun place you've read about, at least not anymore."

I scratched that dream off the list.

It's true. While advertising was once brainstorming a creative campaign, these days, you're a lot more likely to be working off spreadsheets than sketches.

Teachers struggle with lesson plans, report cards, and admin instead of connecting with and inspiring students.

The majority of lawyers are glorified administrative assistants and proofreaders, at least according to the lawyers I know.

Way back in time a cobbler would enjoy the variety and satisfaction of constructing a boot from start to finish and seeing the satisfaction on his customer's face. These days, what was initially sparked by Henry Ford's assembly line thinking has increased exponentially by globalization and complex supply chains. Many workers involved in manufacturing likely repeat the same one or two things each and every day. They are absolutely disconnected from the end product and their customer's eventual experience with it.

> While the economics of this might add up, is it worth each individual worker—a living, breathing human being—losing so much fulfillment and satisfaction?

So What To Do?

1. Become Valuable
2. Communicate Your Value
3. Be Okay Saying No: Trust Things Will Work Out

Where You Are Most Valued

I've heard one complaint more than any other from ENFPs struggling in their career. It goes something like this:

" I love x, y, and z (usually the core part of the job). But all the a, b, c (usually admin and politics) ruins it for me."

Is it possible to have a job with just x, y, and z without all the a, b, and c? Yes, in theory it is, but it isn't common and *it will never be handed to you*. This is one reason I ultimately advocate self-employment or entrepreneurship to most ENFPs, but we're going to stick to the "working for others" side for this section.

> **Understand:** Most people are more worried about getting in trouble than achieving something special. *Most people are closer to paper pushers than innovators.*

This means a typical manager would choose average work without complications over exceptional work with some headaches. Following this thinking, if you do your job at a 7/10 but don't keep up with the admin or ruffle some feathers with your ideas, most managers would happily replace you with a 6/10 who fills out the forms on time and doesn't ruffle any feathers.

You Must Become The 9/10

Imagine you're the principal of a high school. You're responsible for 30 teachers and 700 students. You also have a spouse and kids of your own and are really into ultimate frisbee because that seems like the kind of lame sport a high school principal would be into. It doesn't take the math teacher to work out that you, the principal, don't have a lot of free time.

Now imagine you have a talented teacher who just so happens to be an ENFP. This teacher shows up, is generally liked by the students, and has the odd moment of genius in her classes. Sadly, she also has above average complaints from parents and is always behind on paperwork, if it is ever even done. This causes bottlenecks for your vice principal who is a total paper pusher and ideally would have the school taught by robots whose sole function was to submit reports on time.

Now imagine a new budget comes in and you need to fire 3 teachers. Your people side likes this ENFP teacher and knows the students enjoy her classes but your vice principal, Mr. Spreadsheet, is on your case. On paper the ENFP teacher is more of a headache than the other teachers and you struggle to articulate what value she really brings to the school beyond any other teacher. You're likely going to make one of two choices here:

Either you let the nameless ENFP teacher go or you push back against your vice principal. With the second option you'll likely still need to speak with the nameless ENFP teacher and ensure she gets on top of her paperwork and "tows the line." Whatever you decide, this teacher is not exactly in the best position going forward.

Now imagine another teacher—let's call her Jane. Yes, Jane gets a name because she is awesome. Jane is a walking bottle of hot sauce and doesn't take shit from anyone. Yet, like hot sauce, she manages to be spicy and likable at the same time.

Jane constantly complains about the bureaucracy and often just ignores paperwork. What are they going to do? Fire her? No they aren't because while ignoring the paperwork, Jane has made herself incredibly valuable. Jane has developed her ENFP Superpowers and is incredibly effective at connecting with troubled students. Those students no one else can get through to, who disrupt everyone's classes and cause all sorts of problems: Jane turns them around.

The vice principal is constantly frustrated and dislikes Jane... but he also respects her. He also knows Jane isn't going anywhere.

Once he murmured something about firing Jane for her refusal to keep up with admin work and her insistence on doing things her way. You laughed him down. "The teachers would revolt. Jane is the reason the other teachers can teach; those formerly troubled students no longer disrupt their classes. Don't even get me started about the parents. If I let Jane go, they'd be demanding my resignation 24 hours later."

Jane might not follow the rules and might cause some headaches, but the good she does, the value she brings, outweighs these headaches 10:1. She's made herself essential."

Become Jane and you can write your own ticket.

ENFPs are idealists and focus on positive virtues in others before short-comings. As a result, we often assume there are these perfect people walking about who have all our positive attributes with none of our flaws.

> There is a saying in the business world that a freelancer, such as a designer or writer, can be skilled, on time, and likable. If someone is 2 of the 3, they will always have work. Someone who is 3 of 3 is a unicorn.

 I share this to illustrate a point: Managers are always making trade-offs. No employee is perfect.

If you excel in certain areas, you will be forgiven for your shortcomings the same way a freelancer who is likable and does outstanding work can be late with minimal consequences.

You will drown yourself when you strip your energy from strengths to mitigate your weak spots. You'll still be weak in the weak spots without anything outstanding to make you worth keeping around.

GREAT AREAS FOR ENFPS TO "WORK"

"My mum says that I was born 45, and I do remember at 6 years old thinking that I should be earning my own living." —Keira Knightley

These days, the line between a lifelong employee, staunchly independent freelancer, and total entrepreneur are blurred more than ever. While some people choose to stay entirely on one side, many are crossing back and forth. Some companies, in an effort to cut obligations, prefer to hire freelancers who they basically treat as employees. Sometimes a freelancer will hit a wall they can't climb and take a job for a period of time to get them through.

This section is designed to be as useful for finding a career working for someone else as it is for choosing somewhere to freelance or building a business. Before getting to the list, a few quick explanations.

For the **Who** part, these can't be completely comprehensive; they are listed to give you an idea. There are always more specialties and areas of focus—some even invented by ENFPs.

When It's Awesome vs Sucks is referring to good and bad experiences in essentially the same profession. I have worked with hundreds of ENFPs around their careers. Two ENFPs can have the same job and have vastly different experiences. This usually comes down to the elements I've discussed (What, Who How), the bureaucratic structure of your chosen employer, and the types of clients you serve.

MEDICAL, HEALTH, AND WELLBEING

What: Helping people overcome health issues or reach higher levels of wellbeing.

Who: Doctors, Psychologists, Councilors, Naturopaths, Massage Therapists, Acupuncturists, Personal Trainers, Yoga Teachers.

Why: Ample opportunity for learning and professional development. Your day-to-day is helping others and usually involves a direct person-to-person connection. It is relatively easy to transition from working for someone else, such as at a wellbeing center or clinic, to working for yourself.

When It's Awesome: You're helping motivated clients improve their lives. You're excited about the progress your clients make and look forward to work. Each session with each client is a new experience and welcome challenge. You can end each day proud of your accomplishments.

When It Sucks: You're bogged down in bureaucracy and paperwork. You're stuck with clients who don't have the desire or ability to progress. You keep repeating yourself and your clients blend into one boring mass.

MARKETING, SALES, AND BUSINESS SERVICES

What: You're helping people sell shit. Sometimes it's good shit people need, sometimes it's good shit people want, and sometimes it's bad shit you manipulate people into buying.

Who: This area includes SEO/Ad/Social Media Managers, Website Designers/Developers, Copywriters, Graphic Designers, Marketing Consultants, Salespeople, Sales Trainers.

The roles possibly suitable for ENFPs include:
~~SEO/Ad/Social Media Managers~~, Website Designers/Developers, Copywriters, Graphic Designers, Marketing Consultants, Sales People, Sales Trainers.

I anticipate a few people will see graphic designer or web developer and think "Hey, I'm not doing sales or marketing! I just code or design." Well, chances are, you're only hired so the company can sell more. If you're working on anything to help a company sell (business websites, logos, ads, etc.) and not aware of it, you aren't very good at your job and you'll be replaced by someone who knows why they're hired.

Why: When an ENFP believes in a product, he can transfer a tremendous amount of enthusiasm to a prospect. ENFPs also build trust and connection quickly and can learn to be great communicators, which are all valuable in sales and marketing.

When It's Awesome: You're promoting a product you believe in that makes the world a better place. Most of your work involves using your creativity or people skills such as writing or speaking with people one-on-one.

When It Sucks: You start to question what you're selling or become fully aware it's horse shit. You spend more time in spreadsheets and apps than with people. No one cares about creativity and your numbers are tracked meticulously by a money-driven boss and you're evaluated purely on your short-term performance.

Personal Story: An ENFP friend of mine started working directly with a small startup. She believed in the product and loved the excitement and variety of working in a small company. One day she was finding a warehouse, another day designing packaging, and another day building a community of customers, meeting interesting people all over the country.

She drove sales and growth through community and personal relationships. She found this very satisfying. Everything was going great until it started going *too* great. The startup grew too much and then it all changed. WHAM! The company got investors. Forget community and connections—now she was forced to focus on technical advertising (like Facebook ads) and had to live in spreadsheets. What was originally a dream job quickly turned into a one-way train to burnout that would take her years to recover from.

TRADES & CONSTRUCTION

What: You make people's home or make their home better.

Who: Contractor, Carpenter, Furniture Designer or Maker, Architect, Interior Designer

Why: ENFPs who have a love for design can excel here. Many of the roles have a lot of variety, physical movement, and connection with people.

When It's Awesome: You're working on exciting projects for clients you like. You balance human connection with design and physical creation. Your work is valued and you're earning big bucks.

When It Sucks: You're stuck doing paperwork or behind a computer. You're working for someone who wants it all done their way or you get stuck with a slew of uninspired projects.

In My Experience: ENFPs are much happier in the more physical roles, which include visiting work sites and actually making something. Architects and interior designers relegated to a computer get bored and burnt out pretty quickly.

THE COMMISSION GAMES

What: In theory you're providing advice and guidance on life's big decisions and purchases for people.

Who: Real Estate Agents, Financial Advisers, Mortgage Brokers, Insurance, Sales

Why: These roles can provide a lot of independence and freedom. They're usually commission-only unless you're working directly for a bank, so you have a lot of flexibility with how you work and build your income.

When It's Awesome: You're flying along working with interesting people, helping them build their future and earning a ton of money along the way.

When It Sucks: There are two "it sucks" scenarios here. The first is the paperwork and admin aspect. In theory this can be helped with an assistant, but in practice this is easier said than done.

The second is when your incentives are at odds with the best interests of your clients, which, in my experience, is frequently the case. A mortgage broker might get a bigger commission from a bank that offers slightly higher rates. A financial adviser is close to a big bonus if only they get $100,000 more invested in a certain mutual fund. It's been shown that real estate agents keep their own houses on the market much longer than their clients so they can get top dollar... but since they earn a percentage—say, 3%—it is financially advantageous for them to sell three houses a month at a slightly lower value than two, even if that means each client gets $30,000 less.

It is also common for those who create the incentive structures to provide the moral justification for choosing them, even if it isn't actually in the best interest of your clients. It doesn't take much to give a hungry man the excuse he needs to eat the pizza.

Personal Story: When I finished university, I knew I wanted to work for myself and I even briefly, very briefly, started my own recruiting company to help people find the right career for them (I guess this calling has always been in my blood!). I soon realized I wanted to work for myself long-term, but wasn't yet ready, so I started to look at these commission-only professions as a great way to learn about business, managing my own life, and making some money. I eventually decided on being a mortgage broker. The firm I chose worked closely with financial advisers as well.

My own experience was mixed. On one hand, I could see how valuable we were. As someone who has recently been trying to figure out mortgages in Europe, I wish I could find someone as knowledgeable as I and my colleagues were. We could help just about anyone get a great mortgage and made the whole thing easy. We were also paid our commission from the banks, so the clients usually got a lower rate AND it didn't cost them anything.

On the other hand, one thing we all knew was that RBC, Royal Bank of Canada, would ALWAYS undercut us if a client went in with our mortgage proposal. So in theory, every single one of our clients would have been better off wasting our time than going to RBC. Of course, then we wouldn't exist and RBC would raise rates.

Life is complicated this way.

On the negative side, it became very clear to me that the financial advisers I worked with cared about their clients and genuinely wanted to get them good results, BUT they all had a little Wolf of Wallstreet in them. They took pride in closing sales and maxing out their commissions. One adviser in his 40s had dozens of stories about how the banks and mutual fund companies would reward him with "all-inclusive" nights out. Yes, we're talking hookers, hookers, and more hookers. These are the same trusted mutual fund companies you'll see advertising with a happy family running through a field and a beautiful old couple traveling Europe with their successful retirement funds. I have no idea how widespread this is as I was living in Vancouver, which, as a financial center, is notoriously dirty and corrupt.

Personally, I lasted about a year in that world before I decided I needed to do something else.

ENFP Story: Marshall

Marshall is a father of two and financial adviser living in Phoenix. Marshall ended up in finance after following some familiar advice and was doing pretty well for himself. Financially he was good, but he lost a lot of energy to procrastination and avoidance. Life wasn't bad, but having been married to a J type who insisted her way was always right, Marshall had some work to do on embracing his real self and creating life on his own terms.

Through my programs, ENFP Unleashed and The Free Freelancer, Marshall made a lot of changes, but he loves one particular nugget he learned:

"When Dan encouraged me to stop worrying about how I was supposed to do things and gave me permission to do all my paperwork last minute, which is when I did it anyhow, I found myself with so much more free time.

Since embracing my personality, I've worked much fewer hours, taking a ton of vacations, and yet, also made more money. I've also met my awesome partner, a fellow ENFP, and am having the time of my life."

THE CREATIVE SPACES
AND THE ARTS

What: Content Creation, Theater, Painting, Creative Writing, Music.

All of the above can be done in one of three ways:
1 — For yourself as a pure artist. For example, you paint and sell your paintings or have a creative YouTube channel.

2 — Fully employed. I have a friend who was an actor on a very popular YouTube channel. While it might look like he was a famous YouTuber, he was actually just an employee and actor and felt as frustrated being one as you'd expect.

3 — A hybrid. For example, there was a time when I was writing for clients while also writing my own book.

Why: If you're interested in creative work, I don't need to tell you why you should do it. A painter has to paint and a writer has to write.

When It's Awesome: Dude or Dudette, you're writing / painting / singing for a living! Do you know how cool that is? You're making money doing what you love! People admire your work and pay you well. You have a community of friends in similar pursuits. You're excited and flowing most days.

When It Sucks: Duuudddeee... I gotta write / paint / sing to get paid. People are cheap and no one is paying me what I'm worth. I can't call my mom without hearing the anxiety in her voice when she asks "so honey, how is the art going?" I don't know any other artists. I recently comparison-shopped prices for selling a kidney. Sadly, China's organ harvesting has really driven down prices.

Some Advice: The hybrid approach ain't easy. Despite my attempts to throw in some humor, this book is far from a literary masterpiece, but I've still only been able to complete it by dedicating 90% of my time and 95% of my focus to it. I have tried splitting my time before with little success.

Plus, doing something creative is scary and if you have a steady paycheck, I guarantee you'll drag out your potential public failure as long as possible. As long as there is money in the bank, a book can always use one more revision, an art exhibition just one more piece.

So perhaps it is better to fully work for someone else while developing your craft on the side, save some money, then quit when you have a runway—say, 6 months of expenses in the bank—and go all-in on your creative pursuit.

Personal Story: I have a friend I'm very proud of. She took the leap and moved to Paris to be a full-time painter. She lives in the Montmartre district with her musician boyfriend. She paints. She also sells her paintings for a reasonable sum. So far so good.

I thought she was doing great but when I visited her recently, she said a few things that implied she was stuck in that painful barely-earning-enough-to-live-but-not-dying income zone entrepreneurs and artists know so well.

What was she doing wrong? I put on my business coach hat and started to ask questions. How long does it take her to create a painting? *A few hours to a few days or a week for something huge.* How much do they sell for? Hundreds to thousands. Who buys them? Loyal, repeat buyers. Do most of them sell? How much inventory does she have?

While her mood was a little down while answering, **all the numbers she gave me suggested she could be crushing it.** I missed one crucial question:

"Wait, how often do you actually paint?"

Well," she said, "it really depends on other things."

I sensed a runaround answer but at this point I was a dog with a bone and wasn't going to drop it.

"OK, in the last 90 days, how many paintings have you finished?"

" I dunno, a few.

"How many?"

"Four. But one was really big and took a few days."

Why am I sharing this story? Because as a creative, you can do everything right, but if you miss this one critical deal, you're always going to struggle. ***Playas gotta play and painters gotta paint.***

When you go all in on an artistic pursuit, the universe will present you with a dessert cart of excuses to choose from. Do not even consider the pastries It's time to eat keto. Look away. Close the lid. Throw that cart in the pool or all you'll be doing is wasting away your willpower.

Save that willpower for the one and only thing you should be doing: Creating. If you're a writer, write. A singer, sing. A painter, paint. If you waste your days worrying, second-guessing, and distracting yourself, you'll prove all the doubters right without ever giving yourself a chance to succeed.

COACHES, SPEAKING, AND WRITING: LIFE AS AN EXPERT

What: You build valuable knowledge through learning, application, and experience and use this, with your awesome energy, to make people or organizations better.

Who: Public Speakers, Writers, Coaches, Consultants, Advisers, and Other Experts.

Note: There are coaches, including me, who create a career similar to a therapist or psychologist where they have a practice based on regular clients, mostly by referral. This section is focused on a different kind of coach.

Why: This area can be very natural for some ENFPs. We love to learn, we love to share, and we love to make other people's lives better. It is also an area where you usually are paid based on output, results, or impact versus hours put in, which is very good for us ENFPs who can often produce more in three hours than other people can in eight... but then we need to lay on the beach for the next five hours.

When It's Awesome: You spend your time learning and developing your knowledge and ideas around an area you're extremely passionate about. Your clients love you and you feel more energy at the end of the day than the start. You've chosen the right content medium for your talents and audience such as writing or podcasting. You're giving tremendous value to the world and being rewarded for it.

When It Sucks: You bought some coaching certification without any real idea of what makes you a good coach or where you want to specialize. You're not a grinder and don't want to coach eight hours a day, but you don't have the focus or knowledge to really specialize and offer value, so you get trapped as another broke life coach.

Don't: Be generic. As a freelance copywriter I worked primarily with coaches and specialized in finding their unique personality and appeal and bringing it out in their marketing. I still apply this knowledge and process for my coaching clients in The Free Freelancer. From all this experience I can tell you the value of channeling your authentic personality and gifts. Not only will it help you get more clients, but you'll feel more aligned, enthusiastic, and driven to promote yourself.

Some Advice: Perhaps no psychological term is misused more than "impostor syndrome." I have many videos on YouTube addressing this, which you can find on this book's main video resource page here: www.DreamsAroundTheWorld.com/Calling

But here's the lowdown: Impostor Syndrome is not when you feel insecure about doing something new or don't think you're good enough. Impostor Syndrome is when someone has attained a high level of success—faster than most people and they irrationally feel like they don't deserve it and will one day be found out and lose it all.

The thing people think impostor syndrome is, when you're starting something new and feeling unsure whether you are good enough to succeed is called... BEING A HUMAN.

Sociopaths aside, *everyone* feels this on some level. You're supposed to. Listen, just because you decide you want to go hunt a lion doesn't mean you should trot off into the savanna with nothing but a spear and some positive thinking CDs. Despite what all the people selling crazy expensive programs to achieve your ultimate dreams promise, in any competitive market only a certain amount of people succeed and it takes work and growth to do so.

That feeling, the one saying "maybe I'm not good enough," is another source of fuel to keep you going forward and ensure you *are* good enough. You take one step at a time, improving your confidence with every one, until one day you wake up and you realize "damn, I'm good at this."

ENFP Story: Craig

When Craig first emailed me a thesis-length description of himself and his circumstances, I couldn't help but think "They really don't pay me enough for this!"

Nonetheless, I read his thesis and replied. Soon after, Craig hired me as his coach and then joined my program, The Free Freelancer.

Craig's ENFP intuition was strong. He had a law degree but he knew that wasn't the life for him. When we spoke, he was starting a career in coaching, initially with a focus on voice and presence since he had experience acting and a strong connection with that community.

Craig is a very likeable guy, and being an ENFP in London, had quite a wide community. Yes. Definitely using his ENFP powers.

But here's the thing: Knowing a lot of people and being liked by most of them is only valuable, in a business sense, if we have a clear offer, a service, some way people can help us.

Trust me on this. I have an insane rolodex of contacts and two of my close friends in Prague are famous YouTubers, but aside from some advice and support, it hasn't really ever benefitted my business because I focus on a very specific group.

But this wasn't the case with Craig when he decided to expand his coaching services to include work around trauma and the body. At first, he was struggling and running out of money, terrified he'd have to go back to a part-time telemarketing job he hated and had recently quit. Together on a group coaching session, we created an awesome offer for his new service. Over the coming days, Craig shared this with his friends and bam! Even without a fancy website or big social media presence, he sold out a 12-week program.

Craig did this by using his personality and the connections he had naturally created over the years combined with a bit of hustle and some good business.

After he secured this steady stream of income and didn't have to worry about rent, Craig's coaching business began to take off. Soon he was adding extremely well-paid corporate engagements for large law firms and even Google to his plate and making the big bucks.

Last I checked, Craig is now focused on coaching for the LGBT+ community, which means he eventually learnt the same thing I did: As an ENFP, earning the big bucks is initially exciting, but ultimately it is much more important to work with people you really care about and remain 100% authentic in your message.

Why do you think I'm not doing $10K weekend workshops on personality type for companies or coaching executives? Because my fellow ENFPs are my people and my message is about authenticity, freedom, and purpose. That's more important than extra money in the bank.

Getting a Second Opinion

A few of my most popular YouTube videos are about ENFP careers. Based on the comments on those videos, I can already anticipate the flood of emails: "Hey Dan, what do you think about ________ career for me?"

While I would love to answer these, I am not able to for two reasons: My own time and my responsibility to give you a good answer. I'm sorry catlover1994@gmail.com, but simply knowing your personality type, date of birth, and love of cats is not enough for me to really advise you on a career choice. But I don't want to leave you hanging. So I've set up a page where you can purchase a one-time career consultation with me. Availability may fluctuate depending on my writing and travel schedule, but you can find the details here: www.DreamsAroundTheWorld.com/CallingConsult

ENFP CALLING SUPERPOWERS

You won't need to be an ENFP to spot the pattern in the next super-powers. They're only truly valuable when mixed with one other element.

I'll give you a hint: It's Wallstreet's favorite word right before a financial crisis.

That's right! **Leverage!**

ENFPs are valuable when we use our superpowers to enable other people to be even more valuable.

Think about it this way. If an ENFP learns to become 50% more productive, they become 50% more valuable. If an ENFP can teach 10 colleagues how to be 50% more productive, they have generated a 500% improvement in productivity.

This doesn't dismiss the need for improvements in your own self-management: If an ENFP learns how to become 50% more productive at making others 50% more productive, than I suppose that's at least a 750% increase in total productivity right?

> Do not take on grunt work. You are not a grinder. *Repeat after me:* "My name is ___________. I am an ENFP. I am not a grinder. I will not do grunt work."

A lesson I learned the hard way: Don't call the work you don't want to do grunt work. It has an odd ability to offend partners, colleagues, and employees who are doing this work for you (which they often enjoy).

ENFP SUPERPOWER

THE IDEA GENERATOR

I've heard hundreds of people say something like " I would __________ (start my own business, take a trip, change careers) if I just had an idea about what to do."

I have heard exactly 0 ENFPs say this. Well, except when fear is blinding them. I'll discuss that later in the "Doing Your Own Thing" section.

ENFPs may have shortcomings but coming up with new ideas is not one of them.

Potential Superpower: To spot opportunities and generate new ideas in just about any area of life or business.

Blocks: Not all ideas are good ideas, but few ideas flow when you're focused on only finding a winner. Learn about proper brainstorming methodology and open the floodgates on your creativity before you apply filters to shake out the gold flakes from the sand.

Keys To Developing: That Extraverted Intuition of ours, the function that means we're always looking, learning, and jumping from this interest to that... it comes in handy here. Singular thinking rarely leads to a new idea. Most new ideas come from mistakes or cross-pollination, when wisdom from one field is applied to another. So embrace your love of learning and intentionally take in a diverse range of knowledge.

ENFP SUPERPOWER

THE STARTER

My former partner Gabi was absolutely wonderful. She took life at her own pace and as my mom said, "made me kinder and softer." Quite often, Gabi would encourage me to "slow down and stop being impatient."

I see her point of view…but also I get bored easily, want to do a lot, and hate sitting around wasting time. So there's that.

Chamberlain was a patient man. Churchill wasn't.

If you're not a history buff, Chamberlain was the cowardly British prime minister who encouraged Hitler to take over Czechoslovakia. Churchill is the man who stopped Hitler.

Not all ENFPs are impatient and few are as impatient as me, but almost all ENFPs have a "quicker" relationship with time than others and a desire for action. We are starters and we excel at activating the energy in others.

RUN!

JUMP!

DANCE!

We get people moving and make things happen. We're not afraid to initiate a new project and we're capable of activating the energy in others to really move things forward and get the ball rolling.

This is why, in well-run companies, ENFPs are often put in charge of new projects and initiatives.

Potential Superpower: To take the first steps in starting something new and activating the energy in others to keep it going and growing.

Blocks: Think of starting something as pulling the pin on a grenade. You've taken enough action to guarantee something big is going to happen... now toss it to someone else and make it their problem.

Don't get stuck running and maintaining a project you start. it's hell and a waste of your talents.

Don't try and start more than one thing at once. Starting is intense and demands everything you have to give. Start something, go all-in, and then get out once it's working!

> You'll succeed more by starting four projects for three months each over 12 months than trying to start four projects at once and complete each in 12 months.

Keys To Developing: One way we activate energy in others is by communicating our vision and making it clear what we need other people to do. Practice communicating what you want in clear, concrete language. Develop your ability to apply a healthy amount of pressure on others to get to work and follow-through on their promises to you.

ENFP SUPERPOWER

THE RECRUITER

Having the ability to generate dozens of new ideas and activate the energy in other people to help execute those ideas isn't very useful if you're alone on an island.

Nor is it very useful to have an incredible product if nobody knows about it.

This where the ENFP communication and persuasion strengths can be turned into The Recruiter superpower. Whether recruiting people to join your team or sex cult, or to become an early adopter and customer for your new product, your ability to recruit people to your way of thinking is one of your most valuable strengths.

Potential Superpower: The ability to persuade other people to see your way of thinking and join "your side" when it is something you really believe in.

Blocks: Fortunately, most ENFPs come with a natural safety valve to prevent us from destroying the world: our Fi. Put simply, when we are healthy, we can only promote something we really believe will add value.

Generally, this is awesome, but there is one case when it presents a painful struggle: When you have started your own business. It is totally natural for new entrepreneurs to feel insecure about themselves and their product. The problem is, when you feel insecure about your product because your baby is new and you're still building your confidence, it can be really difficult to sell and promote it and unlock this ENFP Superpower.

Keys To Developing: Practice makes perfect here. I wish there was an easier way, but when it comes to sales, you ultimately need to just get out there and do it. Each time becomes a bit easier.

It is helpful to find someone you can learn from who specializes in selling for NF types as most sales books and training are written for people like ESTPs and ENTJs who love to sell and do fine with rejection. In my experience most ENFPs do best with a consultative selling approach focused on asking questions and listening with a minimum of hard selling and absolutely no cold calling. I've put up a video introducing this concept on the book's resource page: www.DreamsAroundTheWorld.com/Calling/

WHEN ENFPS HATE THEIR JOBS

"When I was 5 years old, my mother always told me that happiness was the key to life. When I went to school, they asked me what I wanted to be when I grew up. I wrote down 'happy'. They told me I didn't understand the assignment, and I told them they didn't understand life."
—John Lennon

Not every ENFP hates their job, but if an ENFP hates their job and the reason isn't obvious, such as an asshole boss, the reason is likely in this section.

If you currently hate your job or would like to avoid hating your current or future jobs, then you may also benefit from reading this section.

If you're pretty sure you never want a job, and want some more reasons why many jobs suck, you will have fun reading this section.

Most Jobs Are Not Like the Movies

I took law in high school and was the head defense lawyer in our mock trial. I was also a fan of The Practice. In each episode Bobby Donnell would always win his cases through some technically legal, not so moral, but undisputed genius move. The show rarely showed lawyers wading through legal documents or burning the midnight oil and yet he always won his cases. This is the kind of job I could excel in.

In the mock trial my client was accused of drug possession with intent to sell. I was given a lot of facts and circumstantial evidence to learn and prepare my case around. But also, I wanted to play Starcraft.

At first, I struggled to choose between winning my case and playing Starcraft, but then I remembered The Practice.

I decided to apply the ol' 80/20 rule and focus on my one and only character witness: The accused's older brother who was a respected high school teacher.

Whether or not I won the case isn't really important. I'm proud of what I came up with and I don't care what anyone said about the mock trial rules: If Chris, the respected high school teacher, had just followed my plan and told the jury the drugs were his then his younger brother wouldn't be serving 10 years upstate.

Turns out even in a mock trial, being a lawyer isn't as fun or easy as on TV.

Sadly, no lawyers I know resemble Bobby Donnell from The Practice. Few teachers are Robin Williams in Dead Poet's Society. As far as I know, Ben Affleck's role in The Accountant is mostly fictional, but I'm still holding out hope.

Few jobs are like the movies and even those that share elements usually involve more paperwork and repetition than we ENFPs would like.

Lesson: TV and movies, as well as the advice of your guidance counselor, can be a starting point for possible careers, but narrow your list down by speaking with real people working in those professions and find out what their day-to-day is like. How do they spend most of their time? Get specific.

Damn You Henry Ford: The Specificity of Modern Jobs

We live in a world where goliath companies, governments, NGOs and charities rule. In these massive organizations it makes sense for employees to adopt very specific roles.

> Unfortunately for the ENFP, more specific roles = less variety and less opportunities for cross pollination.

Compare Microsoft to a small startup with three employees. At Microsoft, the whole system won't work if all of its thousands of workers don't really know what they're working on. It works much better, instead, if everyone has a very specific role with very specific tasks with a clear power heirarchy. There isn't much freedom and flexibility.

In a small startup, on the other hand, there are a lot of fires to put out, and it's a lot to handle for just three people. The fast pace necessitates that each person is flexible and constantly moving in new directions, applying themselves as best they can. Nobody has a fixed role. If they did, the whole business would struggle.

You can probably guess what I'm going to say by now: ENFPs work best in the latter situation. The larger your company and the larger your team within it, the more specific your role is likely to be and the more repetitive your day-to-day work.

The Perks Aren't The Job

All careers have their exciting moments. As a chemistry and engineering student, Andrew, a former client of mine, won a free trip to the American Chemical Society National Conference one year. It was really cool; over 50,000 people who loved chemistry came together in a section of San Francisco to talk about cutting edge research.

Andrew literally watched people get jobs and make post-doctoral connections just by striking up conversations with researchers they found interesting after their presentations. If you went to the bars at night (which I'd always recommend, even if you don't drink), everyone there was a chemist, and you could geek out together and talk about how weird osmium chemistry is, or how cool it is that Einstein's theory of relativity explains why mercury is a liquid and gold is yellow. He even got drunk with some of his professors, but he told me not to tell anyone. (Oops.)

It would be hard not to be passionate about chemistry at a chemistry conference. It's cool to be part of such a unique, specific community, and it's affirming to know that tens of thousands of people are interested in the same things that you are. The conversations and connections you make there are novel, interesting, and fun.

But once again, don't be fooled. Going to a chemistry convention is not the same thing as being a chemist. If you hate going to the lab every day, going to chemistry conventions isn't going to suddenly make you love your job on a daily basis.

Broken Ladders

"Normal" career positions are just too slow for us. Most ENFPs struggle to find the perfect job because we learn fast and get bored. It's both a blessing and a curse.

Driven by our Extraverted Intuition, we're keen on diving fully into new situations and absorbing huge amounts of new information. We thrive at spotting patterns and quickly understanding how things work.

Unfortunately, the rest of the world doesn't always keep up with us on this one. We are the odd ones out.

Typical career ladders usually aim to promote people every two years or so. We're usually bored by then. Assuming that the day-to-day of our job is relatively consistent, we're the types of people that learn 90% of everything in the first two months. That leaves another 22 months for us to sit around, performing repetitive tasks, and get bored.

To make matters worse, it also means that in the months leading up to our anticipated promotion date, we won't be doing our best work—we did it in those first two months, when we learned faster than all of our peers combined. By the time a promotion comes around, we're bored out of our minds. Our bosses will see this and think twice about moving us up.

Many large companies are based on proving yourself and working your way up with little or no regard for personality job fit. Law firms are perhaps the best example of this. To have a chance of becoming a partner, you must slave away for 7-10 years as a glorified assistant. In the process, you learn to grind it out at the sacrifice of everything else.

What makes a good partner? My understanding is the best partners are focused on sales, which includes finding and keeping the best clients, as well as recruiting and keeping the best young lawyers. Call me crazy, but spending seven years buried in paperwork doesn't seem like the best training to be an excellent partner. I'm also not so sure that being an excellent grinder means you have any chance of being a great partner.

Many ENFPs excel at big-picture, strategic work but get bogged down by paperwork and less exciting details.

> Our creativity could flourish in high-level positions but
> to reach these positions we're often asked to grind away
> one of the best decades of our lives.

While this isn't always the case, if you hate your job, there's a good chance it's because you're stuck in this grinding phase where hard work and output are more valued than intelligence, creativity, and strategic thinking.

We thrive, on the other hand, in jobs where we are independent and frequently challenged, like entrepreneurship and freelancing. These positions give us more control over our work and life. As a freelancer, you don't need to wait around for a promotion to start making more—all you have to do is start charging more, either from your existing clients or by finding new ones.

Further, the demands of freelancing and entrepreneurship tend to be fast-paced and flexible. If your turnaround on clients is relatively quick, it means you'll be finding new work and learning about new businesses very often. You never get past that two-month mark where things get really boring; instead, you're challenged to learn and adapt constantly.

To some people, that might sound very stressful. But I believe it's the good kind of stress—the stress that pulls the best out of us without pushing us past our limit. For many of us ENFPs, it's incredibly fun and it's a way to apply our strengths to make the most out of our work. Very few other types could handle the fast pace of freelancing, entrepreneurship, or any kind of self-employment, for that matter. I devoted a whole section to self-employment just because I love it so much.

Once more, this does not mean that you should or shouldn't choose freelancing or entrepreneurship as a career. Instead, focus on finding something that has the right level of challenge for you and understand that a slow-moving corporate job is probably going to bore you unless the day-to-day is very interesting and engaging. Even then, your daily work would still have to challenge you every now and then so that it doesn't become boring.

Bureaucracy and The Wrong Managers

My wine glass is empty so this will be a short one.

If you're working for someone who is:

1. Highly structured and oriented towards rules and processes and

2. Does not respect other ways of doing things...

You are likely to struggle with, if not totally hate, your job. Yes, this includes nearly every government job outside the CIA.

MAINTENANCE PEOPLE VS PROJECT PEOPLE

I am not someone known for my consistent nurturing abilities. For this reason and my love of travel, I used to only own one or two plants, but when Gabi and I moved in together I decided to take advantage of her green thumb and turn my apartment into a jungle.

When Gabi and I broke up, there was some serious concern over the future of our plants. Not how we would divide them but rather concern over the wellbeing of the plants I would inherit.

The idea of consistently watering and nurturing plants never excited me and I knew if I wanted my jungle to survive, I would need to make it interesting.

So I came up with a challenge: How could I get these plants to grow as much as possible over the summer?

Over the next week, I measured luminance, bought bigger pots, and moved plants to the optimal locations for growth. Maybe I could be great at this!

Then winter set in and the same guy who could re-pot a dozen plants and water them religiously during growing season was now forgetting this biweekly ritual. I could almost hear my unconscious say to me:

"What's the point? They aren't growing now. Best case scenario, they just say the same."

It sounds outrageous, but this gave me tremendous insight into just how much I despise maintenance. If something is not growing, if it isn't moving forward, I have no interest. To be clear, this is a Dan thing, not necessarily an ENFP thing, but it wonderfully illustrates the difference between project and maintenance people.

Maintenance people love routine and consistency. Maintenance people can work gradually towards a goal, one percent per day, and eventually get there. Maintenance people are the classic slow and steady tortoise.

Project people may benefit from routine but we love challenge. Project people take on massive challenges and take risky actions to reach their goals, often in one big swoop. Project people are the hares. Most ENFPs are project people.

Maintenance people blog every 3rd day.

Project people write a book every 3rd year.

Maintenance people post a video on YouTube every Tuesday and Friday.

Project people post one epic video every 2 to 11 weeks.

Maintenance people bring their wife flowers on every appropriate holiday, plus every 3 months.

Project people forget about the holidays but buy their wife a Zebra on a random Wednesday because it reminded them of their first date at the Zoo.

Now I have good news and bad news.

Good News #1

Many people with significant accomplishments and contributions to the world are project-based people. Artists go through massive creative booms followed by time off. Entrepreneurs are driven by a big challenge. Heck, even Winston Churchill thrived under the pressure and challenge of wartime, but peace was an absolute bore for him.

Bad News #1

The majority of large corporations and jobs are not designed for project-based people. There are plenty of roles for project people, but they often lack the benefits of being project-based working for yourself.

For example, I can apply my project-based energy to work my ass off and finish this book and then take a month off. At a large company you may get an intense project that challenges and pushes you to be your best, but I doubt you're getting a month off when it's done.

Good News #2

When you design your life to embrace your project-based way of work-ing, the results can be spectacular. Wouldn't you rather work hard for six months a year and take the other six off? Life is a lot more fun, and feels like it lasts a lot longer, when you have different phases, tempos, and areas of focus.

Bad News #2

More and more, the world rewards consistent maintenance work and the pressure is to conform. Social media platforms do not like it if you post irregularly. Instagram's algorithm punishes people who don't use the app addictively. Beyond the evil corporation angle, human nature also rewards consistency. If I follow someone on YouTube, I want them to post on a regular basis.

Good News #3

As of this sentence, you are now the boss of your own life. If you think you're someone who is project based—and as an ENFP, you almost cer-tainly are—then you have the power to change and design the life you'll thrive in.

If you're unhappy in your job, there's a good chance that they want consistent maintenance-type work from you. The external pressure forces you to conform and get it done, but each day, little by little, you're moving closer to burnout. Not to mention you're missing out on all the fun, thrills, and satisfaction of taking on big challenges and totally crushing it working in your natural style.

My editor Tara, an INFP and Author, said it may be worth mention-ing somewhere in here that the frequent release advantage may matter less in the coming years as consumers are flooded with so-so content. She mentioned how in indie publishing, the industry is moving away from the "rapid release advantage" because of the glut of content. "Peo-ple can read a million free shitty formulaic novels, but many of them are craving something legit good."

I agree, and it is one reason that as of this writing, I am changing my YouTube banner from "New Videos Every Week" to " I Publish When I Have Something Valuable to Share". Your time is valuable, and the last thing you need is to invest 10 minutes in a video created solely because someone needed to "make content" to feed the corporate algorithms.

Wired For Freedom

Project people are much better suited for creative and entrepreneurial pursuits which just so happens to be the subject of our next section.

CHARTING YOUR OWN COURSE

If it is the right time and fit for you, there is no better choice for an ENFP to maximize their freedom, ~~gelato~~ growth, and potential for contribution than going your own way.

DOING YOUR OWN THING

"There is nothing like a dream to create the future."
—Victor Hugo

I'm done pretending all paths are created equal. There are many respectable and intelligent reasons for an ENFP to get a job, including getting the training and growth needed to go at things solo, and I've met ENFPs who have totally rocked it working for other people but...

If you've got what it takes to make it work, there is no calling more suited for an ENFP than doing your own thing. Nothing else gives you the freedom to design your work around the life you want, the flexibility to design your work around what you do best, and the opportunities for exponential rewards when you do great.

Does this mean every ENFP should start working for themselves this very moment? Absolutely not. Working for yourself is an intensive journey that requires facing many fears and faults and often requires going through a few challenges and even failures before getting it right. In some cases, you're better working for someone else as you develop yourself and the skills needed to go at it on your own.

One could even say the same thing Hank Moody once told a writing student: "If you can do anything, anything else, do that."

Like writing, working for yourself or doing your own thing in any capacity, isn't always going to be easy, but once one tastes the sweet nectar of freedom and satisfaction it dispenses, they never want to go back.

ENFPS AS ENTREPRENEURS

> "I think the person who takes a job in order to live—that
> is to say, for the money—has turned himself into a slave.
> —Joesph Campbell

I might be a little biased, but I think entrepreneurship, or at least entrepreneurial-minded work, is the long-term calling for most ENFPs.

It's certainly not for *all* of us, at least not immediately. There's a level of mental fortitude and work ethic required to be a successful entrepreneur that isn't a universal ENFP trait and must be developed. For those who learn fast, love a challenge, and are willing to work hard and flex their creative muscles, I can't imagine a job nearly as well suited or satisfying as the one you create for yourself.

You'll Never Be Bored Again

I haven't been bored in a decade. Really. Occasionally, I feel a need for a new challenge and some excitement. So what do I do? I change things up and take on new challenges, like when I hosted my first in-person event, Life Design Fiesta, in Mexico in 2018. It was made extra exciting by a red alert on Playa Del Carmen due to excessive cartel activity!

It's Not Easier. It's Different

When you work for yourself, you say goodbye to one kind of stress: that nagging dread that's extra punishing because it exists beyond your control. Someone else is pulling your strings. It's often coupled with thoughts like " I don't want to get out of bed today," "I'm happy I'm sick," and " I can't wait for this day to end." It's the chronic stress rats feel in a cage or we feel when we're working for external rewards and validation with little autonomy.

You trade this dread and angst for another, better, stress: That of complete autonomy and total personal responsibility.

Personally, I thrive in this environment. I believe in my own ability to perform more than I believe in any company, and I get more certainty working for myself than for someone else. But not everyone does—at least, not initially.

> If you're someone who loves blaming others for your place in life, don't even think about entering this race. But if you're a go-getter, **there's nothing better than being the captain of your own ship.**

It will take time to develop, especially if you've been crewing someone else's ship for a while, but with time, your confidence and belief systems will change.

By the way, from a health perspective, the kind of autonomous stress you feel as an entrepreneur is infinitely healthier than the handcuffed dread-fueled stress one experiences when they feel trapped.

Is being an entrepreneur the right choice for you? Let's go through some bullet points.

Pros of Entrepreneurship for ENFPs

► You are 100% responsible for your own results.

► You have infinite room for growth.

► You get to learn new things all the time and count it as working. For example, I've recently studied cinematography for my YouTube channel.

► Provided you don't quit and that you complete your trek through hell, you'll become one of the most self-aware and insightful human beings there is. Eventually, people will be like, "Damn, you totally have it figured out" and you'll cruise through life with a calmness and self-confidence few people ever experience.

- You get to set your own hours and develop your own schedule... meaning you can totally take a 10 a.m. break and eat gelato on a Tuesday.

- You can make a lot of money.

- You spend a lot less money on clothing, commuting, emotional eating/drinking/shopping, and taxes.

- People are likely to admire and respect you.

- Done right, your business can give you total location independence, and as an entrepreneur, it's extremely easy to get visas to most countries.

- You can be a more awesome parent, partner, son, daughter, etc. because you can adjust your schedule for your loved ones. Having time and location freedom means you can take a three- to four-week trip with your mom, brother, or uncle, as I've done five times so far.

- It's more stable than a job.*

Cons of Entrepreneurship for ENFPs

▸ You are 100% responsible for your own results.

▸ You might face some adversity from friends and family. It's taken about 10 years, a healthy income, and having my own team for all of my family members to accept and respect what I'm doing.

▸ During your early years, a comment as simple as "how's your business" will dredge up every insecurity you've ever experienced.

▸ You probably shouldn't take a 10 a.m. break to eat gelato every Tuesday.

▸ If you're quitting a cushy corporate job, it will likely take around a thousand days to fully replace your corporate income as profit.

▸ Eventually, people at your co-working space will wonder why you only own one pair of jeans. They won't buy your whole minimalism argument.

▸ If you don't utilize your Te (Extraverted Thinking) and create structure, your work hours can become all hours.

▸ People may assume you're actually unemployed, or in the best case, an Uber driver.

▸ If you don't set firm boundaries or work outside the house, people might see your business as a hobby and walk all over your time.

▸ It's less stable than a job.*
  *It really depends who you ask on this one.

Text Message
Today at 19:21

Mom

> HOW'S LIFE? HOW'S BUSINESS?

> WHAT THE HELL, MOM? YOU NEVER BELIEVED IN ME. YOU DON'T UNDERSTAND HOW HARD IT IS SOMETIMES. YOU AND DAD AREN'T ENTREPRENEURS. YOU DON'T LOVE ME. ALL MY FRIENDS THINK I'M A FAILURE AND I SHOULD BECOME A TOUR GUIDE. I'M TERRIFIED ABOUT PAYING RENT NEXT MONTH. SOMETIMES I CRY.

Mom

> THAT'S NICE, HONEY. AND HOW IS YOUR GIRLFRIEND? IS SHE DOING WELL?

Are ENFPs Natural Entrepreneurs?

Yes.
And no.
Umm… sometimes.

Let's look at both sides.

ENFP Entrepreneur Qualities:

▸ We don't like being told what to do.

▸ We have lots of ideas—often good ones.

▸ We take action and get things started.

▸ We love to create.

▸ We're great at marketing, sales, and getting people excited about a new way to do things.

ENFP Notpreneur Qualities:

▸ We can struggle with giving orders and clear direction to other people.

▸ Before we get a grip on it, we can be awkward about confrontation or discussions around money.

▸ We get bored easily.

▸ Some of us aren't willing to push through the tough times required to come out on top.

Alright, so at this point you've heard me mention ENFP Unleashed a few times. This program includes 12 training sessions. One of these sessions is specifically about ENFP entrepreneurs and, because I write better with wine, I've impulsively decided to share it with you. Honestly, if you've made it this far in the book, you deserve a reward.

You can access the training, which is about an hour, at this link: www.DreamsAroundTheWorld.com/CallingEntrepreneurs

Let Me Give It to You Straight

I've been working for myself since I was 10. I've had failures and successes, big and small.

It is interesting to compare my experiences with my friends from college who mostly went on to become lawyers, consultants, and doctors. I don't think any are ENFPs, but it's still a revealing comparison.

Between university graduation and age 32, roughly 2006 to 2016, I imagine most, if not all, of my friends from college earned more money than me over a 10-year cumulative total. I had some great years, but my friends were professionals working 50-60 hour weeks and consistently bringing home the bacon.

But money isn't the only way of looking at it. During this period, my friends would, at best, have had 2 weeks of vacation each year. Me? I was living the retirement they were saving for, travelling the world and taking at least a few months of vacation each year.

During this period, I imagine my friends have experienced relatively consistent stress and the odd bit of dread from their high-pressure professions.

The stress of an entrepreneur is very different. I'm fully responsible for myself, and often others. I rarely feel dread or that powerless stress because I'm always in control, but with that control comes serious responsibility.

Most of my friends have bought homes and all of them have made some serious returns on their real estate investments, since Vancouver prices always seem to rise.

I haven't made millions, but I *did* spend the pandemic quarantine living in million-dollar villas and having one of the best years of my life.

I can also take a whole month off whenever I want to with just a few weeks' notice. But when I need to, I will work all hours. For example, it's 9 p.m. right now and here I am, working. I was up at 8 a.m. this morning and have been burning the candle at both ends to finish this book and keep up with my growing company. At the same time, my new videographer is in town and we're trying to film 20 videos this week—all while my mom is visiting. Still, it's my responsibility to keep up with my writing, and I have been.

As you might imagine, I've also increased the number of massages I get and drinks I ingest this week to keep my sanity.

But I love all of it.

I think tonight is a perfect example of the entrepreneur's path. No, I'm not out with friends or binging Netflix, but I am drinking some nice wine, listening to amazing chill-hop, and writing, which I love doing.

Like I said, working for yourself requires a higher level of responsibility and a different kind of internal engine.

You need to want to produce. If your goal is to sit back and do nothing, entrepreneurship is not for you. I'm here to create something, and I love giving it my all.

I've made the spreadsheet and I can show you the numbers. I could easily tweak my company to run on autopilot. I could work five hours a week and earn six figures. I could set it up in a few hours and it would run flawlessly.

But I'm not going to because I have a motor and I love to create as much as I love to serve. I'm here drinking wine and writing because you're here (hopefully) drinking wine and reading.

ENFPs care. We want to make the world a better place and I'd be lying if I told you the opportunity to make the world better was equally split between employment and entrepreneurship.

If you really want to have the biggest impact, create the best lifestyle, and challenge yourself while growing more than you ever imagined, being an entrepreneur is your path. It isn't for everyone, but if it is your calling, I salute you and will always support you as best I can.

Motivation

There is one thing that has always helped me take risks and move forward: Having something I want that's so awesome I'll climb any mountain to get it.

For me, one of these things is being location independent, and that's what we're going to explore next.

Of course, if the ability to live and work wherever and whenever you want doesn't appeal to you, if you have no desire to explore new cultures and meet people from around the world, then you can always skip that one. Also, please hand in your ENFP membership card at the front before you leave.

LOCATION INDEPENDENCE

"I can't wait to get on the road again..."
—Willie Nelson

I'm writing this from the courtyard of a craft beer bar in Brasov, Romania.

It's been, well, more than a few days since I wrote. My last saved file is from Timisoara, on the other side of the country.

Sometimes I find it tough to get myself into "work mode" when I'm traveling. In my current case, it took a few days of consistent good sleep and a very well-planned day.

Having to work during a vacation is, well, stupid. It isn't something I regularly make a habit of. Despite being location independent and living in lots of interesting locations, my life is not a "vacation" in the traditional sense, since I run my business from wherever I go. But I also take vacations that are actual vacations: No laptop, no work.

In this case, my ambition collided with my vacation plans and I decided to challenge myself with some challenging writing goals which collided with a road trip with my Mom. I wouldn't do it again, but if it all works out and you're reading this, I'm glad I did it.

Being location independent is the ability to live and work from wherever you wish, mostly whenever you wish.

I prefer this term over the popularized "digital nomad."

Digital nomad is a prescriptive term: You're likely some 28-year-old programmer or remote worker and you must be "nomadic" because it's a sexy word. Being a digital nomad means having the ability (and often being forced to due to visa or financial issues) to constantly move while working. In my opinion, that isn't the most ideal lifestyle.

I've met many digital nomads in Europe who are glued to their computers during American working hours (evenings in Europe). You can't exactly claim to have lived in Europe if you've been glued to Zoom every night. I've met plenty of other digital nomads who are limited to the cheapest countries to fit their tight budgets.

What Is Location Independence?

Location independence doesn't mean having a job that lets you work wherever—it means having the resources to fully determine where and when you work.

In my case, this sometimes means 60-hour work weeks. It also means I have the ability to work just 2-5 hours a week and maintain a significant part—sometimes all—of my income. If I didn't feel called to my work and mission, that's probably what I would do.

Location independence could mean living on a cheap beach in Southeast Asia, living on the Champs-Elysees in Paris, or in Shinjuku, Tokyo.

It is all about choice.

Whenever possible, I believe all ENFPs should strive to have as much location independence as possible. Some callings don't jive well with it, including some that involve the most meaningful and impactful connections. While I'm able to help just about anyone transform their skills or knowledge into a location independent business, I don't always advise it.

I've hesitated to encourage my personal trainer to do this. He's fit, healthy, happy, and spends his days doing work he loves. We train remotely via a video call, but most of his clients are in person. I don't think he would be happier if he was on eight video calls a day with less equipment and limited options for helping clients.

Another option for him would be to share his expertise via some kind of social media platform or paid products. He is certainly capable, and perhaps one day he'll go down this route. But I've debated if all the extra work would ultimately be worth it for him.

Should I Try to Become Location Independent?

A few years back I created a detailed video series that walks you through the process of becoming location independent with your own business starting at absolute square one.

You can watch it on the book resource page as long as you promise not to judge my hairstyle or video quality. Seriously... I need you to promise.

Today I speak with a lot of ENFPs interested in moving abroad or spending a few years traveling the world while earning a good income working for themselves.

Pros and Cons of Location Independence for ENFPs

Let's first look at setting yourself up to have the ability to live and work where you want. This list overlaps a lot with the pros and cons of entrepreneurship for ENFPs.

Pros of Location Independence:

▸ Forces you to develop a high level of self-awareness and discipline.

▸ It's one of the ultimate freedoms.

▸ More relationship options.

▸ Ability to be there for those you love when needed.

▸ Friends envy you, which is usually enjoyable.

▸ Great deals on trips, vacations, and experiences during off-peak travel times.

Cons of Location Independence:

▸ Requires a deep level of personal responsibility (entitled victim-minded people need not apply).

▸ There may be times that require you to work harder and longer than others.

▸ Often involves difficult conversations.

▸ Sometimes encourages "There's always something better" syndrome and discourages looking within for solutions.

Moving Abroad

So let's say you're on board with this location independent thing and you have the ability to move to a new country. Is it a good idea and when should you do it?

I will indulge your rational mind with some logical reasons to do so, but the TLDR is YES. Yes you should move abroad, at least once.

When should you do it? This answer is different for everyone. Personally I moved to Costa Rica before my business was flourishing and the experience helped me grow my business and ultimately transformed my life in ways I would have never predicted. For many people moving abroad can help create the environment needed to make big life changes. I was one of these people.

Pros of moving to a new country:

▸ Time slows down. Seriously, this is one of the coolest parts. A year lived between three countries lasts a lot longer.

- You expand your friend groups.

- Family relationships tend to improve with an ocean between you.

- You'll expand your perspectives and turn worldly knowledge into worldly wisdom as you experience different ways to live.

- You're able to grow and evolve faster than when surrounded by the same people and peers you grew up with.

- Other countries are really cool. Even Romania, with all of its orphans and vampires, would be awesome to live in for a year or two.

- Your dating life will likely improve.

- The country-specific benefits of where you move! Whether it's the sunshine and friendly vibes of Costa Rica, the food and wine of Italy or France, or the beer of Prague.

Cons of moving to a new country:

- Making a cons list here would be disingenuous. It would be me pretending I see any downside in making a move, which, actually, I don't. I am 100% all for it.

I left Canada in 2012, have lived in nine countries since then, and have spent significant time in quite a few others. The experience helped me grow as a person in unimaginable ways. I've understood the world in new ways, gained new perspectives on myself and my own culture, and developed intellectually. From a lifestyle perspective, well, it has been tremendous. I absolutely love everything about it.

So, if you've been thinking of trying a move abroad, should you do it? How do the pros weigh against the cons?

You should, with 100% certainty, always do it.

Almost every choice is reversible and this is especially true with moving abroad. If it turns out that it isn't for you, you'll be one of millions of people who spent a year or two abroad, learned a lot, made lifelong friends, and then chose to move back home. For a worst-case scenario, that's not bad at all.

You can ignore your worried Auntie: You won't need Liam Neeson to come rescue you from terrorists and kidnappers.

I won't list cons but I will list some requirements. These are areas of struggle to watch out for if you decide to make a new country part of your life—which, again, you totally should.

Oh, and don't you dare throw any excuses my way about your mortgage, business, or family as reasons you can't make this happen (if you want to).

Homes can be rented out. Businesses can be optimized to work without you. Kids tend to flourish with travel and new experiences.

If you insist on making excuses, I'll have to tell you about a client of mine who owns a thriving farm and is still moving halfway around the world. I might also remind you of Christine, the woman I met in Rwanda with her 4 sons. So don't you dare for one minute think this section is only for 20 or 30 somethings with no attachments.

And let's not talk about age or fear either or I'll embarrass you with stories of my mom backpacking South America alone in her late 60s or the trip she is planning to East Africa, now in her 70s.

Now, back to my advice on things to prepare for if you're going to try out this living in a new country thing.

Losing Your Foundation & Losing Yourself

We ENFPs are fiercely independent adventurous souls. Yet, our ability to be adventurous is often grounded in a foundation of family, relationships, and community. When you know you have great people to support you, it's easier to feel free and take risks.

Like with vitamins, we're often blind to the effects of our foundation as long as we have it. Perhaps we can be away from our friends or family for a few weeks and not notice anything. But like a vegan who doesn't supplement, you might feel great for your first few weeks or months, but eventually, you'll start to fall apart.

Relationships, routines, and habits that once held you together are now thousands of miles away.

So it's important to create a new foundation, as well as stay in touch with your old one, as you travel. If you move to a new country, join a sports club or organization based around an interest. It could be painting, improv, interesting sex stuff—whatever you're into.

Don't wait until you settle in and the loneliness hits—join something as soon as possible. Speaking of which...

Loneliness

ENFPs have an abnormally high combination of Extraverted and introverted tendencies. This gives us a lot of versatility. I can happily explore a new city or spend a day or two alone, but eventually I'm going to miss high-quality human contact.

There are a few practical ways to deal with this:

- Start creating a new community as soon as you move somewhere. Join classes and communities of fellow expats and locals.

- Date. As a foreigner, you'll be extra appealing and should have no problem lining up a few dates a week. Name one other activity that guarantees a few hours of interesting conversation and the possibility of a lot more. I'll wait.

- Set up regular video calls with friends and family back home.

- Before moving, consider the friendliness of where you're going. The locals in some countries don't speak much English, while others do. Some cultures embrace small talk and lots of people will enthusiastically ask you where you're from and why you're there. Others, well, less so.

Generally, the sunnier and more isolated the country, and the less dictators they've had, the friendlier and chattier people are to strangers. *This is not an exact science.*

In places like Italy and France, people are nice enough, but don't expect anyone to be particularly blown away by the fact that you moved from America to work remotely in Paris. People have been doing that for hundreds of years.

Forgetting Your Responsibilities and Treating It Like A Vacation

Perhaps the most common downfall of new location independent travelers is treating their experience as if it were a temporary vacation. They want to see everything, do everything, and make the most of each day because they're used to having 2-4 weeks of vacation each year.

When faced with a choice to explore a nearby town with some new friends they met or stay home and finish some important work for a client, they're going to choose to explore the town. Because after all, they're on vacation. They may never have this opportunity again.

The weekend comes around, and they have the chance to go out and make a splash. Well, of course they'll go out. Why would they try to get more sleep? They're here to make the most of it, not to rest up or do work!

The problem with this approach is that in order to make your freelancing or personal business work while being location independent, you usually need to put in even *more* hours and focus for the first few months to prove to clients that you're as good (if not better) than you were when you were back home. You need to spend this time building the systems and processes to make sure your business can succeed. So the last thing you want to do in this early stage is treat it like a vacation.

Mindsets For Location Independence Success

These days, there are hundreds of YouTube channels about being a digital nomad. Many are created by, in my mind, people who:

- Are in their first year or so, with a stable job back in their home country that probably won't keep them on remotely forever, so they're trying to sell you some e-book to avoid moving back to Wisconsin.

- Can't actually afford their lifestyle. The amount of people sharing "digital nomad" advice who live off their partner's income or savings they have from back home is really disgusting.

I've been location independent for 11 years. During this time, I:
- Have never borrowed or been given money, aside from the odd birthday gift.
- Have never taken a job.
- Have never "met" a "fan" from Instagram in Dubai for a "modeling event."
- Most importantly, have never had to move back home because I ran out of money or otherwise hit an emotional wall.

I guess you could say I've got this location independence thing down. Want to know how I do it? Here are my rules for starting—and STAYING—location independent:

Act As If You'll Live This Way Forever

Prioritize your business ahead of tourism because, if you pull this off, you'll be able to tour the world until you inevitably start pooping yourself. Yes, I'm keeping that joke alive.

During my first few years of being location independent, I was always walking the line between enjoyment and business success. I consistently prioritized my business so that I could keep going.

I said no to a surfer lifestyle in the dreamy Nosara to live in Santa Ana, Costa Rica, because Santa Ana offered better internet and cooler temperatures. I lived in Bologna and never visited Rome because I needed the little money I had for my business. I've lived in Germany three times and I've still never been to Oktoberfest because I had other priorities.

Now, I don't want you to think there isn't plenty of fun involved in location independence. I've had dozens of amazing adventures and trips when business was good and circumstances allowed for time off—I just didn't force them when I knew my business needed my time and attention.

Like being an entrepreneur, being location independent does *not* mean that you never have to take responsibility. Much the opposite.

Avoid Tourists and Lost Souls

Another good mindset, especially for your first time being location independent, is to avoid the lost souls and the people out on vacation.

We've already established that *you're* not here on vacation—you're here to build a life full of freedom from today until your last breath. The last thing you need to do is get tangled up with people who are either on a quick vacation, trying to make the most of every minute because they have no other responsibilities, or those lost souls who aren't really sure what the heck they're doing in Europe or Southeast Asia while working the odd gig or living off their savings or loans.

As an ENFP, your peer group is incredibly important, and the people around you are going to have one of the biggest impacts on your behavior. Hanging out with people who are in a totally different place with totally different priorities is a recipe for disaster.

Create Community and Bring People Together

You might ask, "Well, Dan, I've just moved somewhere new. I don't know many people. I'm getting lonely and I really don't fancy spending another weekend alone. So what the heck do you suggest I do?"

That brings me to this tip, which has been a game changer for me. One thing I found in many places I've been, especially Prague, is that there are a tremendous number of high quality, inspiring, and awesome people who know very few other high quality, awesome, inspiring people. One of my gifts to the community in Prague has been bringing these people together.

Whether it's organizing a night out on the weekend, my annual Halloween party, or many events in between, I've made a conscious effort to bring interesting people together. In doing so, it not only creates more experiences for me, but it also gives me a chance to contribute and become a valued member of the community.

I've been reminded over these past few days that I've been missed very much in the years that I've been away from Prague. People there have sent some very kind words to me about that, and it's a great way to feel like I'm an important part of a community.

ENFPS AND SHINY OBJECT SYNDROME

"The most valuable of all education is the ability to make yourself do the thing you have to do, when it has to be done, whether you like it or not."
—Aldous Huxley

Because ENFPs are so creative and fluid in our perceptions we aren't quick to label something a failure. Instead of writing off a failed project or deleting that half-written manuscript, we often just add something new to our plate. Quite often this happens when we enter a more difficult phase of our current project or aren't getting the results we want.

So you jump to greener pastures and initially find some positive emotional feedback. After all, what's more fun for an ENFP than starting something new? The early parts of a venture involve more brainstorming, excitement, learning, and even progress. FUN!

Eventually you get to the point where things begin to level off a bit, some sort of plateau, and it's here when the cycle often repeats itself.

The next thing you know, a year or two has passed and you find yourself looking back and wondering, "What the hell did I actually accomplish over all this time?"

This is called shiny object syndrome.

This syndrome isn't unique to ENFPs—most people do this in some form but ENFPs are much more prone to it, and the most gifted of types in denying it is actually happening. The key here is that as ENFPs, we don't fully acknowledge the change in direction. It's all done very subtly, and we justify the way our minds process these changes.

The problem with this dabbling and constant change is that it eats away at our chances of success. We're competing in a world of INTJs. You know INTJs? They're consistent, focused, and dialed in to what they're doing. How are we going to compete if we are in a state of constant change?

I'm sure if we were to search for ENFP blogs, we would find the highest number of blogs started and not finished of any group on the internet. This is, of course, because we like starting. As ENFPs, we get excited about newness. We like things that are novel, we like variety and new challenges. That first part of a project is always more exciting than the last part. But without the right systems in place, we are pulled in different directions, never accomplishing anything.

For now, the most important thing to understand is that shiny object syndrome is often the result of someone choosing the second best option. Of course you're going to change jobs every 6 months when you pick a job you're not excited about. Of course you're going to bounce from one relationship to the next when you settle for a partner you're not all too excited about. **So step one for defeating shiny object syndrome is to raise your standards.** Once you do that, you can apply some of the strategies discussed in the next section

Causes and Solutions For Shiny Object Syndrome

Perhaps there is no problem for which ENFPs receive the worse advice from other types on how to solve as shiny object syndrome. If "just stick to one thing" and "focus better" hasn't been the silver bullet you've been hoping for this chapter will shed some light on why shiny object syndrome is so common for ENFPs and what you can do about it.

Perceptions of Time

The first thing that really helped me figure this out was changing my perception of time. We all have different perceptions of time. For some people a minute can feel like a long time; for others, a week or even a year is nothing but a small blip. I'm sure you have met people who had the same job for 10 or 20 years, and to them, a year is nothing.

I have a friend with a perception of time that differs greatly from my own. When we talk about planning holidays, he's planning two years ahead. I plan my trips a month in advance—maybe two for something big.

On a recent ENFP Unleashed coaching call, I asked members two questions. You might have some fun answering these for yourself, as well as asking people you know.

1)What is a "long time" for you?

2)What is a "short time" for you?

We had some good laughs at the variety of answers, even among ENFPs. You can have some fun first answering these questions for yourself and then asking friends and family.

In my discussion with ENFPs the shortest short time was in the minutes, while the shortest long time was a matter of days. I'm not quite as quick on the draw, but my own times are fairly quick too. As I get older, I become better at having a longer term vision, but I still find it difficult to imagine a gradual, multi-step plan. Why not have it all NOW?!

Well, that's what my unconscious might be screaming but my higher mind has learned this isn't a great way to go. I've managed to reign in this natural tendency and now allow myself to plan weeks, even months, ahead.

As ENFPs, we tend to have an urgency in our behavior. We like to do things quickly and we want instant results. This is good in many ways and it's a real strength in allowing us to drive projects and initiate things. Other personality types will take a year to start their business. An ENFP will start it in a week on a hunch and just go for it. The problem is that our perception that results should be timely often drives us off course.

A few months into something, when we haven't gotten the kind of results we've expected, we start to think "this isn't working." As optimists and idealists, we expect good things to happen quickly. When they don't, we end up changing our minds or thinking "okay this isn't working. Let's try something different." The reality is that things take time. Especially in the new world, in terms of the internet, things take a long time.

You might think this is a contradiction. Isn't the internet about making things quick and easy? The internet is about making *consumerism* quick and easy. But if you want to build a successful YouTube channel, blog, or podcast, for instance, it takes a long time to break through all the noise. If you're living in a small town and you start doing public speaking, you're probably the only person doing this, so it's easy to gain momentum and get a following right away. However, if you start making YouTube videos, it might be a year before you get any real traction because you're now a small fish in a much bigger pond.

Slow is Smooth and Smooth is Fast

There's something that I learned in motorcycle school that really stuck with me. Slow is smooth and smooth is fast. My instructors explained that many riders have a sense of urgency and they try to force the ride. But that's not the right way and doing this makes you a terrible rider. In fact, slow subtle movement makes you smooth, and by being smooth, you're actually faster.

If you look at the best racers, the people who are the fastest, they're the people who have slow, smooth movements. So I started applying this thinking to my life. Rather than thinking about one week at a time and short-term success, I started thinking longer term and having more of a drawn-out goal, realizing that it takes time to get there.

I have some friends who've done very well in terms of their YouTube channels and getting a lot of success. I've watched them from the beginning, initially putting in months of work without results. But they persevered. I know if that were me, I would have quit. I would have thought "this YouTube thing is not working." I've done that in the past. Seeing how much work was required for my friends to succeed changed my perception of time and really helped me in this area.

In terms of applying this mantra to your life, you need to start actively thinking about the idea that slow is smooth and smooth is fast. Realize that you don't need to be successful or achieve your goal in, like, a month. It may take six months, a year, or two years, but that timeframe is still pretty good. Start focusing on that longer-term goal, keeping in mind that it takes time to get there.

As ENFPs, our high expectations and over optimistic views can often lead to huge disappointment and ultimately quitting. If we reframe our thinking and focus on the long-term goal, the big picture, we're less likely to be led by our emotions. We won't react to every bad day or negative event, and we're more inclined to see a project to completion.

When you spend time working really hard on something and you don't get instant results, you're not going to be as disappointed because you're coming in with the mindset that slow is smooth and smooth is fast. Results take time.

Accountability

One thing that can help with this is having some form of accountability in terms of goals and planning.

As ENFPs, we are very good at lying to ourselves. It's not uncommon to hear someone use the old "Its full of antioxidants" excuse to justify eating a block of chocolate or drinking a bottle of wine. ENFPs are masters of doing this with everything. If we want to change direction, we can always find a way to do it, even if it's not the right thing to do.

When we commit to starting a business, we work on it until something happens that makes us feel bad and we want to quit. We will then find a dozen ways to justify this: "Oh the economy changed," "oh I had this job offer," but we're really just quitting because things were hard.

I encourage you to set down a concrete destination or goal. Write it down and share it with someone. Hold yourself to it. Say "this is where I want to go." If you start to lie to yourself and change direction, just be aware that your excuse is a lie. You're lying to yourself about it and you're letting your emotions take over.

Write down your destination and then let it sit for a week. Think about it, really commit to it, and in committing to it, *commit* to it. Don't just scribble something down on a piece of paper one day on a whim. You're probably not that likely to really commit to an emotionally made decision. Try to make your choice really concrete and then stick with it. That's going to help a lot with changing your perception of time and staying on course.

Get Your Fun Somewhere Else

One last little tip. If you are an ENFP, you have a need for variety, excitement, and newness. You will need to find other ways to meet this need outside of your career or business. This may include playing extreme sports, traveling, or training for a marathon. Whatever it is, find something that will satisfy that desire. When you meet that need for excitement in other places, you might not need it in your business, career, or personal life.

This applies to all areas of your life. If you don't intentionally, proactively meet your need for excitement, you'll unconsciously meet it through more destructive ways. So you can choose to do things that are novel that will bring you excitement and put you in charge of your own life. Or you can leave it to your unconscious to meet your ENFP need for excitement. Just don't be surprised if you end up doing things like fighting with your partner, always switching who you're dating, or constantly changing your business direction. So I really encourage you to proactively meet that need for newness rather than just let it happen to you.

One Foot After the Other

Left, right, left, right... just keep walking.

It was 35 degrees in Spain and I was carrying way too many groceries. It seemed, once again, that my eyes had desired more than my back could comfortably carry.

I'm a little stubborn, and the wait for a taxi was quite long, so I committed to the walk. I just kept telling myself, "one step at a time." If I had stopped to imagine just how far I still had to walk with all these groceries in this intense heat, I likely would have curled up in a ball. That's why I didn't. That is why I trained my mind to just focus on each step, one at a time.

This is the same thing I have trained my mind to do in business. With an adventurous life and vibrant business there is always something I could be distracting and stressing myself with. If I was intent on feeling horrible in any particular moment, I could utilize my Ne and just start cycling through all the to-dos and what-ifs, imaginary and real. That would likely lead to me curled up on the sofa in that now infamous overwhelm-induced fetal position.

That is why I don't.

I say to myself—literally, speak to myself—"One day at a time. One foot after the other." If I am writing, I am writing. I am not thinking of this email or that, the projects I'd love to do in 2024, or even how I am going to edit, illustrate, or market the book I'm currently writing.

I just write. One word after the other. One key at a time.

I've realized that many of the things I am most proud of came from really focusing on one thing until it was finished. I allowed myself to be present and work on something, one step at a time, until it was finished.

When we ponder too many options or obligations at once, we unleash a recipe for overwhelm. To look into the future and see a mammoth ice wall staring back at us. We think "surely we can't do ALL these things at once." We turn our ambitions into an impossible feat. We get scared. We retreat.

In these moments we even forget the old cliches like "Rome wasn't built in a day."

Our skewed sense of time simultaneously imagines EVERYTHING we will need to do over months or even years, and then, in a truly unfair fashion, compares that list to what we could act on that day.

The next time you find yourself going down this path, immediately interrupt the pattern and just say to yourself, "one step at a time… left, right, left, right… one step at a time."

YOU GOT THIS

Making a change is never easy but fortunately for you, ENFPs have Yogi flexibility and Honey Badger courage.

THE ESCAPE PLAN

While I'm focusing on work related change here, this also applies to all big life changes whether ending something that isn't working for you or starting something wonderful.

Making what you think will be a dramatic change is not easy for anyone. I have quit jobs, ended relationships, and moved countless times. I am the king of "in theory dramatic, but in reality, usually goes smoothly and everyone is nice" changes and still, I know how difficult it can feel.

I want you to know there are many forces working against you. These forces are working to maintain the status quo and keep you stuck in place. These forces are so vast that I am literally writing another book on them, and it is becoming massive.

> I share this with you because you should never feel guilt or shame about your past inaction. You must accept that the past is the past and change is hard AND your future is still 100% in your control.

In my experience, in the majority of cases, completely ripping off the band-aid beats band-aid solutions.

Ripping off the band-aid hurts for a moment and then it's done.

Band-aid solutions cover up the wound without fixing anything.

People habitualized to avoid a few moments of pain and change are experts at adopting band-aid solutions. Popular options include:

▸ Working from home a few days a week.

▸ Taking an extended vacation.

- Raises and other perks.

- Buying something expensive you now need to pay for.

- Experimenting with alternative relationship styles.

Note: Of course, many of the above can be a positive thing if there is no wound you're covering up. If you're honest with yourself you'll always know if you're polishing a prized possession or a turd.

Let me repeat: It is almost always less painful to take decisive action and make a clear break so you can move on, but to do so in a responsible, kind, and caring way.

If, due to fear of confrontation, you let something build for too long and then explode, you will have experienced months or years of suffering, and then cause a significant amount of pain when a volcano of resentment and animosity finally pushes you to take action.

A firm decision contemplated over a few weeks or months is better. For example, according to a psychologist I spoke with, when ending a long relationship it's best to be decisive while giving the other person some hints and having some discussions so they can mentally prepare. Do not blindside a boss or partner; this robs them of their sense of control.

Well, unless they're a bit of a psycho. Then it might be best to blindside them and get the heck out. But this is rare, and ENFPs often assume a confrontation will be MUCH WORSE than it actually is because as we avoid it we let our imagination run wild and develop the worst-case scenarios in our minds.

"Have You Thought Of, Oh I Don't Know, Being Honest?"

No further explanation necessary. Marina understood.

Marina is a high-performing ENFP killing it at her day job and building an awesome yoga studio on the side. She was complaining about how she keeps getting promoted and handed more responsibility. After breaking from coach mode and an obligatory mention of the classic Seinfeld episode where George tries to get fired but keeps getting rewarded, we dove into it.

Her boss asked about her goals and she gave a less-than-truthful answer that definitely did not include her yoga studio or our work together growing it.

"Why not tell him the truth? You have a lot more power than you think," I told her. I put on my tweed jacket and lit my imaginary smoking pipe. *It was story time...*

I met Andrea in Argentina in 2008. A group of about ten of us walked from our hostel to a local bakery for takeaway food. By the time Andrea and I ordered, everyone else had left and the sheets of rain outside were impenetrable. We were trapped inside until the storm decided we could go. While nothing romantic ever happened between us, I will admit our initial meeting really was the picturesque start of a rom-com.

I learned that Andrea was a fellow Canadian spending the majority of a year slow-traveling around South America. Full on traveler, DSLR, black and white photography, blog and all... She was all in her quit-my-job-and-see-the-world adventure.

She told me she had been a marketing manager in Toronto. She was great at her job, but the combination of stress and meaningless work wasn't doing it for her, so she quit. Everyone gave her the same old "this is a big mistake," "you're ruining your career," yadda yadda yadda. Her company even offered her all kinds of perks to stay but Andrea trusted her intuition and followed through.

By the time we met, her old company had offered her more than double her previous salary to return. Doesn't exactly jive with the "throwing your career away" narrative she was told before quitting, does it?

She said no and continued her travels. That's a confident and courageous person for you—or maybe just a stubborn one. Either way, she stuck to her guns. To nobody's surprise, I later learned that Andrea was an ENFP.

Did Andrea end up marrying a Latin musician, taking up surfing, and living out her life on a Brazilian beach? Is it Andrea on the cover of this very book?!

No. Well, as far as I know. After her travels, she took some more time to figure out her next steps. Last we spoke, she had moved to Miami, a compromise city that filled her soul with the Latin energy she loved so much and allowed her to keep speaking Spanish. She eventually took another job, and I'm sure another after that, and I am confident each one brought her closer to her calling. I'm also confident that she has never forgotten what she learned and now lives with the power of knowing she can walk away at any moment and will be just fine.

I finished recounting this story to Marina.

"Marina, you're in a niche technical field, you're a natural leader, you have a crazy level of drive, and you're great at your job. Plus, hiring is a pain in the ass and replacing you would cost your company a fortune. In your country, it's nearly impossible to fire someone without cause, and ultimately, you do want to quit soon, at least if the job stays the same...

"So why not put your cards on the table? Ask for x, y, and z. If the management is rational, they'll do the math and realize it's better to keep you and accommodate your requests in return for your continued high performance and hitting your targets. And if they're irrational, well, you always have labor law. Worst case scenario, they fire you and you get what you wanted anyway."

I was pushing Marina to have that conversation. You know the one I'm talking about. That dreaded conversation. The one where you honestly say what you want.

Gasp!

We ENFPs hate confrontation. We dread that conversation with a partner, boss, or even employee where we lay it out and say what we really mean. We often prefer to live in ambiguity on Planet People-Please.

If you let this fear dictate your actions, you'll lose in life. Your employer (unless they're me) is unlikely to go out of their way to give you extra vacations or encourage you to find better work-life balance.

You're going to have to fight for what you want.
 I have good news, though. By "fight," I literally mean just have a civil conversation where you say "I'd like this please."

While I love ripping band-aids off, perhaps you can also just start with an honest conversation with your employer or partner to get the ball rolling. You can share how you feel and what you're experiencing and learn about their perspective without having a dramatic outcome in mind. At least, they'll know your concerns and be better able to adjust for you, or better prepared for the news when you decide to rip that band-aid off.

If only there was a way to play with our perception of fear and use this to change our patterns and take charge of our motivation levels. Well, perhaps you'll find something like this in the next chapter.

ICE CREAM & WHIPS: HOW TO MAKE A CHANGE

> "Fearlessness is not the absence of fear. It's the mastery
> of fear. it's about getting up one more time than we fall
> down."
> —Arianna Huffington

This forms the basis for all human—likely all mammal—behavior. If something causes us pain, we avoid it. If something gives us pleasure, we pursue it. There you have it, the mystery of human nature solved in a single paragraph!

> Understanding your own relationship with pain and plea-sure is a secret weapon for developing your ability to take on uncomfortable situations, make big changes, and ulti-mately create the life you want.

Don't pop the champagne just yet. *How* we calculate pain vs pleasure is where life gets complicated. Let's take the three-minute cold shower practice, for example. Few will argue that a cold shower is inherently pleasurable. Yet, many do it, myself included, and sometimes even grow to enjoy those three minutes.

Why?

I calculate the pleasure I'll receive throughout the day from the mood and confidence boost. While those three minutes will suck, the plea-sure I receive throughout the day outweighs the three minutes of suf-fering. Knowing suffering will end, and that it contributes to having a better day overall, actually makes the cold shower less painful.

I discovered something similar growing up in Canada. No matter how rainy, how cold, if I opened my chest, lifted my chin, and put a big smile on my face I would feel warmer than assuming the "curl up and hide from the cold" position. Try it.

I could dissect the details of this for years, but to keep the trees safe I'm going to focus on the three most important aspects of the pain vs pleasure equation.

How You Weigh Pain vs Pleasure

Everyone weighs pain vs pleasure differently, but as a species, humans avoid pain more than they seek pleasure because we are wired for safety and certainty.

Here is a thought exercise:

You go to a new restaurant and they present the meal. You have two choices.

Meal One: You will be served a perfectly acceptably average dish that you will neither throw up nor remember.

Meal Two: We will flip a coin in the back deciding whether you are served the best meal of your life or will spend the night over the toilet.

Which meal do you choose?

I didn't intend this while writing the above exercise, but we could make a few tweaks and we'd have how many people choose to live:

Option One: You will work at a perfectly acceptably average job that will neither satisfy nor destroy you. You will not be laughed at or admired because you will not be remembered for anything.

Option Two: You'll roll the dice and pursue your calling. You might face some struggles, hardships, and rejections or discover a level of connection, fun, and fulfillment you always dreamed of. OK, you'll probably experience both.

The Math of It All

My dad has been trapped in is a pain (risk) oriented pattern for a long time. He will avoid something that could be 8 points of pleasure because it might, *might,* cause 4 points of pain.

> This fear averse behavior is amplified because he overestimates the odds of something bad happening and tends to experience less pleasure from a positive situation than other people.

Then there is how he interprets a bad situation. For example, imagine you're traveling and your flight is delayed so you get stuck overnight somewhere. My dad might describe this situation as " a total nightmare" whereas someone else might describe the same situation as "It was cool. I got a free night at a nice hotel in the airport and met some other travelers from the flight."

Someone who is pain-averse, who imagines every uncertain situation as " a total nightmare" and overestimates the odds of the negative scenario occurring is unlikely to take any big risks in life.

On the flip side, someone who really enjoys their great experiences, has a realistic—even optimistic—estimation of the future, and finds a way to make the best of unfortunate situations is going to be exponentially more likely to take risks in life. Each risk they take will build their confidence and ultimately enable them to follow their calling and create their ultimate life.

How You Weigh Intensity vs Duration and Present vs Future

"A coward dies a thousand times. A hero dies but once."
—William Shakespeare

Is it better to be punched in the face a couple times and be done with it or to live in fear of a bully for a couple of months?

Intellectually, I know it's better to take the punches and be done with it but nobody told my 14-year-old self this fact so I learned a cycle of avoidance from a young age.

I'm not the only one whose experienced this preference for slow drawn-out torture. Many people choose to live with low level dread 24 hours a day for years rather than having one somewhat uncomfortable conversation with their boss or partner.

If you currently have a low-level pain of 3 or 4 every day, it will be very difficult to muster the courage to face a temporary painful situation of 7, 8, or 9 to eliminate the long-term pain.

What you want to do is change how you perceive time and pain: It is easier than you think.

Sit somewhere quiet and close your eyes. Well, finish reading this part, then close your eyes.

Now what you're going to do is think about the ongoing painful situation and let your imagination run. See the situation today, tomorrow, next week, the week after. See and feel the pain you'll be feeling EVERY DAY. Now keep going into the future and start to imagine what this pain is going to do to you if you don't change. See beyond the daily dread and unhappiness: Feel what happens when you start to face health consequences from the stress. When you lose friends and family who can't take the unhappiness. What does it feel like when you look back from the future with intense pain and regret over all the years you've wasted because you didn't trust your intuition and make a change?

Follow the above process a few times and I guarantee your perception of pain and pleasure will start to change. You'll understand in your bones the insanity of experiencing pain at a level of 4 hundreds of times to avoid one experience at a 7, 8 or 9 is ridiculous.

WHY FOLLOWING YOUR HEART IS THE MOST LEFT BRAIN MOVE EVER

" I don't have a plan B because it distracts from Plan A."
—Will Smith

There is no one more dangerous than the well-spoken, hyper rational, left brainer who thinks they understand the world. The left brainer excels at dissuading anyone who might dare to stray from the average in an attempt to maintain the accuracy of his statistics derived from the average.

If you can plant enough doubt in a new entrepreneur with the ol' 9 out of 10 small businesses fail statistic, you're guaranteed to maintain the accuracy of this very statistic.

> For all the traveling I've done, I can tell you the absolute worst place I have ever been, a place I wouldn't wish on my worst enemy, is two places at once.

If you want to guarantee failure, spend the majority of your time questioning what you're doing instead of doing what needs to be done. This way, you can avoid the work that would make you successful and maintain all your relationships by proving your doubters right.

People love to be right.

Reason #1 To Follow Your Heart—Ignoring It Isn't Possible

Telling an ENFP to ignore their heart is like trying to train your dog to ignore that bucket of KFC you've left at the edge of the table. There might be a window of time when it looks like things are going as planned, but eventually and inevitably you are going to get stuck with one hell of a vet bill.

Trying to follow the so-called responsible advice of well-meaning but entirely uninformed friends and family members will feel right in the moment. In fact, you'll likely feel a big surge of relief when you first decide to ignore your heart, your dreams, and your calling and follow the safe path.

> This wave of relief is known as "abdicating personal responsibility." It's the same relief you feel when your co-driver takes over during a road trip or you're in the presence of an authority figure who tells you, "Everything is going to be okay. Just relax and let me handle it".

This desire for Mommy and Daddy to take over and tell us everything is going to be okay isn't inherently wrong, but it certainly isn't going to guarantee a happily ever after. Just ask the Russians how things worked out when Uncle Stalin said, "just let me make all the decisions for you and everything will be alright." Weak people love to hand over their lives to Chairman Mao, Adolf Hitler, or that friend working at a bank. Anyone who is willing to tell them, "Just go with whatever everyone else is doing. No need to worry your pretty little head questioning the purpose of your life."

According to Abraham Maslow, whenever we pursue something greater than ourselves, or even attempt to improve ourselves and "move up" in our own lives, we will feel a high level of apprehension, tension, and resistance. This is normal, and trusting yourself to move past it is one of the greatest growth experiences you can have.

Cowering to external pressure, while undesirable, relieves this tension. Like a baby coddled by Mother, you feel a welcome wave of relief.

The only problem is you've just set yourself up to be a 40-year-old who still shits his own pants.

Or her pants. As a feminist, I firmly believe women are just as, if not more, capable of running from their dreams as men are.

Author's Note:

If you enjoyed these last few paragraphs it is worth noting that 15 minutes ago, I felt this pressure to leave the table from both the restaurant staff and my own internal resistance. I was reaching a section I knew would be difficult to write and I felt a strong desire to turn off, pack up, and move on. I didn't. I kept my ass in the chair and, I think, produced a nice little collection of paragraphs above. Just a fun little behind the scenes for you.

So running from your calling can produce a welcome feeling of relief, but then what?

Then reality seeps in. For some, it hits that first day in the office, whereas others last six, 12, perhaps even 18 months before the familiar dread trout smacks them across the face. If you ignore your heart, it will come back and bite you. It might not be today, it might not be tomorrow, but it will make its opposition known. You might start feeling restless at work. *Maybe you get a sinking feeling in your stomach every time you wake up and realize you have to come into work.* Perhaps you start fantasizing about the awesome life you ran from.

This is when the ENFP makes a change. Whether they make that change immediately or indulge themselves in years of denial is a personal choice, but eventually they will quit and find themselves... well... at the start of this chapter all over again. Some will finally go for it while others will, once again, embrace the comfort of conformity... until that lil ol' heart speaks up again.

Now I'm not one to care about CVs, resumes, work histories, and the like, but I would think that if you're trying to be successful in the traditional professional world, it isn't so easy with a scattered disaster of a CV. And if you aren't even going to succeed in the corporate world, wouldn't you be a lot better off just going for your dreams in the first place? At the end of the day, you're going to have more money and peace of mind continuously working away at something you love as opposed to the up and down cycle of torture, despair, and conformity ignoring your heart is guaranteed to generate.

Reason #2 To Follow Your Heart: It's Your Best Chance at Succeeding

On the other hand, if you just happen to be feeling rebellious, you could throw yourself into something and find out what you're capable of when you dedicate 100% of your being to it. To appease all those left brainers in your life, let's do some simple math on why this is not only the best way to go, but the only way.

1. Let's assume you have 100 points of energy to spend each day. This energy is a combination of your passion, enthusiasm, cognitive abilities, and focus.

2. Everyone else also has 100 points of energy.

3. As you build success in any area, you need to use less energy to achieve the same results as someone starting out because of experience, knowledge, and connections.

4. Like an RPG character, it is possible to apply (rebuffs) that drop your amount of energy and (potions) that temporarily increase it.

Some common rebuffs include:

- Splitting your focus between two things: minus 20% energy while activated.

- Splitting your focus between three things: minus 40% energy while activated.

- A long stretch without a win: minus 15 points until win.

- Pondering if you're on the right track and questioning everything: minus 80 points for 3 days.

- A not-so-supportive conversation with a doubtful friend or family member: minus 50 points for 3 days.

Some common potions include:

- Having a big win: +30 energy points for next 7 days.

- Obsessive focus on one thing: +50% energy while activated.

- Support from those inspired by your dedication: +30% energy.

- Hard deadlines and no turning back: +50 points until deadline.

Imagine Bob splits his focus because he wants a plan B. He drops from 100 points to 80. Bob then delays his chances of reaching a big win and loses another 15 points. The lack of success triggers him to question his purpose, which wipes 3 whole days off the calendar... further delaying a win. Shit, now it's Sunday and Bob has his weekly call with his father. No wins to report and Bob can hear the disappointment in his father's voice. There goes three more days. Thinking he might be off track, Bob decides to add in a third pursuit to "hedge his bets," but instead of doing so, he drops his daily available energy to just 60 points **total**... that's only 20 points for each pursuit... before all the other rebuffs he is bound to face. No wonder he isn't getting anywhere.

Then we have Betty who goes all in on one thing. She's instantly at 150 energy points compared with Bob's 80 or 60... but really it's 150 versus whatever percent of energy Bob puts towards any one pursuit. Betty's friends were initially critical and anxious for her but now her dedication has become a source of inspiration and her friends and family are her biggest fans +30%. Damn, at this point Betty's points are so high, she's checking off big wins every week or two, adding evening more energy. After a few months, Betty is rocking with 200+ points of energy per day focused on a single magnificent outcome. No wonder she's having no problem crushing Bob and his measly 8 points of energy he can dedicate a day.

I'm not even going to extrapolate this out two to three years when Betty is getting 10x the results for each bit of energy she invests because she will be crushing Bob on an astronomical scale.

FACING FEAR AND TRUSTING YOURSELF

" I don't have a plan B because it distracts from plan A."
—Will Smith

Unfortunately, convincing your left brain doesn't make following your heart much easier. We're wired for security and it will take more than a few chapters in a superbly well-written and utterly hilarious book to rewire years of fear-based thinking.

Trust me, I'm still working on it and I'm the handsome, funny (and, if anyone is asking, single) bloke writing the damn book.

Nevertheless, addressing our left brains is a good start and something you want to begin conditioning today. Realize that any logical decision maker, whether it is part of a person or a computer, is still only making decisions relative to the information it has.

> If Einstein doesn't know the floor is lava he's going to get burnt. An AI system created with inputs from a religious cult or communist state are going to make very different "logical" conclusions.

Two smart people can disagree because they've developed very different underlying beliefs which determine what "logical" conclusions they come to.

It follows that examining your underlying belief structures and, when necessary, adjusting them to better match the kind of life you'd like to have can have a profound impact on your life.

In our lives we come across statements that are so powerful, so profound, that a single exposure clarifies our world and changes us forever.

"You can tell what a man really thinks about you by the earrings he buys you." —Truman Capote
"When you're single you date other singles. When you're a couple you date other couples." —Nora Ephron
"We don't stop playing because we grow old; we grow old because we stop playing." —George Bernard Shaw

 I do not presume any such statements are to be found between these pages. If you beg to differ, feel free to heap your praise my way on social media or in a glowing review, but assuming I'm not the second coming of Christ, you're going to need to do some work to make these new insights stick.

When you read that Will Smith quote at the start of the chapter, what did you think? Probably, "This Dan guy needs a better editor. He used the same quote a few chapters back".

At this point you've read that quote twice. *You have about 4,562 more times to go before we'll be equal.* I extracted that audio from a Will Smith interview and listened to it on repeat thousands of times. My mind became a Reddit bot triggered whenever I heard the phrase "plan B" or "backup plan"; I would instantly hear Will Smith in my head saying " I don't have a Plan B. It distracts from Plan A."

We're all programmed from the day we're born. Some people grow up with perfect parents in a perfect community and are programmed with the exact belief system needed to accept themselves, utilize their personality and superpowers, and create an awesome life. If you aren't one of those three people, you better get used to reconditioning yourself because there ain't no other choice.

Reconditioning does not need to be a complicated process. It starts with awareness, which you now have, so check that box off.

Next is identifying the beliefs that might be holding you back and coming up with a new belief to replace them. In my Will Smith example, the old belief was " I should have a plan B in case things don't work out." The belief I wanted to replace this with was, "There is no need for a plan B because it distracts from plan A." The reason for adopting this new belief is right there in the new belief; having extra plans is distracting.

I once created a custom track for a friend of mine. It is basically four minutes of me telling her how awesome she is and instilling new beliefs in her. Since then she moved from Canada to India and became one of the country's top photographers which lead to was mingling with Bollywood's most elite. She mentioned to me she shared the track with one of India's biggest Actors who thought it was awesome.

Yes, when she told me that I seriously considered moving to Mumbai and becoming a guru to the stars but alas, with my sensitive lungs and food allergies I wouldn't last a week.

Why am I telling you this? Oh, right. I've decided to make you a collection of tracks just like this. it's your call if you want to listen to them every morning on a walk, run, or at the gym, or mix them into your days another way. You'll can find them on the book resource page: www.DreamsAroundTheWorld.com/CallingAudio

Making Friends with Fear

By the way, you might be wondering why I am dedicating so much time to discussing fear and beliefs here versus the meat and potatoes of self-employment. Well, the first reason is that building a successful business requires a wealth of knowledge beyond what any one book could include. Trust me, I've tried to find, and even to write, "the one book" I could give to people and it doesn't exist. Building your own business requires a lot of different reading and usually some kind of training or coaching as the cherry on top.

The second reason is that, well, knowledge is not what is initially holding anyone back.

"Dan, I'm not afraid. I just don't know what to do. Tell me the right business to start and I'll do it."

"Dan, I have no problem taking risks and following my dreams. I just don't know how taxes and business rules work. That's why I haven't started."

LIAR!

Fear is a sneaky mother fucker and rarely attacks head on. Fear loves to drum up seemingly legitimate excuses to keep us in place and protect our delicate egos. No one starts off saying "I'd love to pursue my dreams but I'm just being a coward." First, because this would feel horrible. Sometimes fear works to protect our self-esteem. Secondly, fear often influences us at such an unconscious level we're unable to fully identify our dreams and reach some dramatic showdown or moment of decision because we aren't aware there is a decision to be made.

It is much more effective for fear to blind you from the possibilities early than to risk a direct showdown. I've been helping people identify their dreams and go for it for almost 20 years and I can tell you that once someone is clear on their dream and realizes only fear is holding them back, they are just a few steps away from realizing that dream. Fear knows this too and so puts up many obstacles in advance to prevent this clear and simple showdown.

By the way, we're all susceptible to this. Last week at a BBQ I was hosting, all my friends collectively insisted I needed to be doing stand-up comedy. "The shit you say randomly is funnier than anything I saw at the open mic." "You would absolutely crush it."

And I know they're right. Outside of professional comedy circles, I can't recall ever being the second funniest person in a room. So when was my last stand up performance?

Never.

While I've never denied I want to do it, I've generated all sorts of excuses around the timing. "What if it hurts my business?" "I'm not sure if a coach making obscene jokes and telling ridiculous stories is the best look." I don't think I want to be a full-time writer or full-time comedian because I love variety and I believe coaching and uplifting others is one of my highest callings. It probably balances out the depression and alcoholism that tend to follow writing and comedy careers.

Even when we have conquered fear in one area of life, faced self-doubt, and pursued our dreams, we need to be ready to tackle it again and again; the process of growth never ends.

Fear is not your only obstacle and reconditioning isn't your only tactic. In fact, this topic is so vast, it is the focus of another book I'm writing of considerable length, but I will do my best to keep things brief and actionable here.

The following are 3 of my favorite ways to handle fear.

Peers

Changing your peers is one of the most powerful ways to change your belief systems. If everyone around you faces down fear and pursues their dreams, you're going to be the weird one if you *don't* and that's a lot easier than being the weird one if you *do*.

Look for people on the path to, or who already do, the kind of incredible things you'd like to do and use that ENFP charm of yours to make them part of your life.

One Step at a Time

This book was supposed to be finished somewhere between two years and two months ago. Sometimes progress is slower than we'd like. Many mornings I begin to feel this nervous anxiety as I neglect other areas of my life to finish this book. It is trying to distract me. I take a breath and remind myself that finishing this book is my top priority now and I can only write so many words a day. I am on the right track. All I can do is take one step at a time, which, in my case, means to sit my ass down and write each day. The absolute best way to derail things is to let my anxiety-fueled imagination explore all the other things I could be doing right now.

Our shorter perception of time makes ENFPs more susceptible to this kind of impatient anxiety. Develop the ability to calm your mind through practices like yoga, meditation, and directed self-talk, and remind yourself you can only take one step at a time.

20 Seconds of Courage and Extreme Accountability

I stole this one from Matt Damon who was cool before he started pushing crypto for quick cash. In the movie "We Bought a Zoo," he tells his daughters the story of meeting their mother.

"Sometimes all you need is 20 seconds of insane courage. Just literally 20 seconds of embarrassing bravery and I promise you something great will come of it."

I've applied this many times to make big changes in my life, combining it with extreme accountability.

How The Process Works

First you identify what you want to do. Perform a standup show, launch your business, do work you love, date someone special, get healthy. Whatever it is.

Second you clarify one action you can take that will permanently rewrite your future. This is the kind of thing when, once you do it, there is no turning back. Here are some examples:

- Ask someone out / declare your feelings.

- Tell your boss you want to quit.

- Pour out all your alcohol—even the expensive stuff.

- Declare a year of keto.

- Sign up for a half-marathon.

- Buy a plane ticket.

- Hire a coach/teacher/personal trainer and prepay for 6 months of sessions.

- Join some kind of training program, community, or mastermind that will force you to show up.

I've done everything on this list and a lot more. For some, you'll want to attach a level of extreme accountability: When I declared a year of sobriety, I promised to move back to my parent's house in the suburbs if I had a single sip of alcohol that year. The moment I made that declaration, I knew I wouldn't touch alcohol for a year.

Other actions, like hiring a personal trainer and paying for 36 sessions in advance, or dropping a large amount of cash on a personal development program, had the accountability built into the action.

Remember, at this stage you are only identifying the action you could take.

Third you prepare and get everything ready. Do all the research, check flights, write the resignation letter, whatever it is. Prepare so it all comes down to one single action you can complete in 20 seconds such as clicking send on the email, "buy now" on the plane ticket or coaching package, or "post" on your declaration.

During this, and previous, steps do not think about actually doing it which can summon up fear, instead pretend it is all just an exercise.

Fourth is your 20 Seconds of Courage. You know what you need to do and all you need to do. This is a great time to use your creativity and, dare I say, make it a glorious celebratory moment. Whether you want to drink champagne, burn incense, or crank out your favourite music—or all of the above—is up to you.

**Create the moment and follow through. Then
celebrate your ass off.**

Author's Note:

I got goosebumps as I did my final check on this chapter because...guess what? Come on, guess!

Two weeks ago my friend, a member of my inspiring peer group, asked if I wanted to come watch him perform at a comedy open mic night. Without even knowing it he had created the environment for my 20 seconds of courage. That's what great friends do.

As soon as I walked in the door I knew what I needed to do. I was terrified, and drank way too much tequila, but I did it!

And, not that it matters, but I was pretty funny.

There you have it. You've now changed your future. If you'd like some examples of how I did this, I've put together links on the book resource page, www.DreamsAroundTheWorld.com/Calling, including how I quit my job without quitting using a time travel trick, moved to Costa Rica and begun my journey to live in 5 countries before I turned 30, and how I started my freelance writing business within 48 hours of deciding it was what I wanted to do.

WHAT'S THE WORST THAT COULD HAPPEN?

"All men die, but few ever really live." —John Eldredge

Like so many people I work with, after a few coaching sessions with me, Andrew quit his job to pursue something better.

He didn't know what he was going to do instead; all he knew was that his current job as a nuclear engineer wasn't a good fit. He knew something else was out there, and he couldn't sit still until he found it.

"What's the worst that could happen?" I asked. "You can always take your old job back and pick up where you left off if, heaven forbid, things don't go as planned." (Spoiler alert: they never do, but that's a good thing).

Quitting your job is a good example of a big decision—an important change that will throw you into unfamiliar territory and turn your life upside-down. Some ENFPs struggle with these choices, either making them too readily and being impulsive, or not making them often enough and settling for a boring life.

I recommend that, like Andrew, you go all-in on pursuing your dreams. But I also recommend that, regardless of your decision, you don't get stuck halfway. Either make the decision or don't—in or out.

Going all-in and committing to a decision forces you to focus and work. It pulls the best out of you, not because you *want* to be that way, but because you *need* to.

In the case of quitting a job, financial freefall is a pretty damn good motivator to start making some money. Andrew quickly pursued and found some new income streams to support himself, and within three months, he was in the black again as a freelance writer—something that, I might add, he had no experience with. But he thought he'd be good at it and it was something he wanted to do.

Less than a year after quitting, Andrew was making more than he did at his old job, gained complete control over his schedule, became location independent (we'll have a chapter on that later), and was happier and growing faster than ever.

The Runway

Your runway is how much time you have to go in a new direction. For example, if you quit your job, how long would you be able to support yourself? If you want to dive into a new career, how long will it take for your new work to support you?

You can make some preparations to lengthen your runway. You can save up cash to cover the cost of transition; plus, you can take some steps to make that cash go further by lowering your expenses—for example, by cooking for yourself or not going out as much (temporarily, of course). You can even line up clients for your new work before you quit your current job.

In other words, you're still allowed to have a plan while you're fearlessly chasing your dreams. It's possible, perhaps even wise, to do both. Perhaps being committed to your dream *might* mean staying in the job you don't like and saving up for a few more months—if that's what it takes for you to finally leave it.

So how long does your runway need to be? Long enough for you to take off, of course! It depends on your risk tolerance, the situation you're in, and the change you're pursuing. Before quitting a job, I'd recommend saving up a few months of living expenses at a bare minimum, or having some business income already.

Basically, it comes down to the math. I've taken on new ventures quite a few times, and I go heavy on cutting my expenses and bringing in new income as quickly as possible. This is what has allowed me to work for myself exclusively since I've been 24. I never once needed to take " a job" despite changing my focus many times and, until my 30s, I never had any savings. This has included periods where I was essentially a full-time freelance writer, a full-time coach, and a full-time author, although for much of the time, I blended three to four interests like I do now: writing, coaching, teaching, and hosting a YouTube channel and podcast.

I don't recommend risking so much that you can never try again if you fail, although I'd be lying if this wasn't my own personal approach. You need to know your own limits and relationship with stress and failure. If you're as big of a Rocky fan as I am, you know you'll always be able to get up and go another round.

So full disclaimer: I can't guarantee that everything will work out. But what I can guarantee is that if you genuinely want to make a change to become a better and happier version of yourself, you'll tap into more power than you ever knew you had. You'll find a mysterious force pushing you along in the right direction.

And I can guarantee that, although those transitioning months (or years) may be stressful, the fire you build in them is worth far more than money, and it's something you can never lose.

Freedom Comes Unexpectedly

As his new writing business started taking off, Andrew was shocked to wake up one day and realize how much freedom he now had. Freedom hadn't been his goal; he just wanted a job that fit well for him. But along the way, choosing to follow his heart gave him flexibility in his life and greater confidence in his decisions—and at its core, that's what freedom really is.

New opportunities inspired new ideas, and he realized that if he could afford to live in America while working remotely, then he could move almost anywhere in the world. When he asked me if he should move abroad, as many of my clients do, of course I told him to go for it. What's the worst that could happen?

Like everyone I encounter, part of Andrew was afraid and part of him was excited. I simply told him, as I'm now telling you, to lean into the excited part, and let trust and time take care of the rest.

He stopped trying to make decisions based on fear, and he started asking the *right* question.

"Where do I really, genuinely, want to go?"

Andrew moved to Thailand, and after traveling throughout Southeast Asia, he still lives there now, almost two years later. Business is good, he's in the best relationship of his life, and he's experiencing a fascinating and wildly different culture. He even speaks Thai—never saw that one coming! All in all, things turned out far better than just okay, and a whole lot more interesting than if he had simply continued as a nuclear engineer for two years.

When we feel the itch to make a big change, the first step is often the hardest to take. But that one step can lead to a completely different life, with unexpected discoveries and joys that ripple even many years after the decision itself.

The Stakes

High risk yields high reward. I see it over and over again. So why don't people just jump in, take risks, and commit to big changes in their life?

Fear.

I mean, duh.

But let me ask you something.

Have you ever said to yourself, "Oh, I sure am glad I never went for that thing I really wanted!"

I don't mean sleeping on a big decision for a few nights, which you should always do.

I mean, do you ever feel good about risking *nothing*?

On the other hand, looking back, how did you reach your biggest accomplishments? The things you're most proud of. How much time, effort, stress, and/or money did you put in, knowing full well that it might not pay off?

Lay it all on the table and jump in when you feel that itch. You know the one I'm talking about—not just *wanting* something, but yearning for it with every ounce of your body for weeks on end, imagining a different world and longing for it to exist.

That kind of itch doesn't just go away. You have to do something about it, even though it probably scares the hell out of you. And for that, there's an important follow up: What's the worst that could happen?

It's true that sometimes things don't go your way. It's true that Andrew just got out of the hospital with the worst food poisoning of his life. It's true that I went bankrupt and that I was completely broke when I moved to Costa Rica on a whim.

But it's also true that he doesn't regret coming there at all or eating those "local-style" raw shrimp, that he feels more alive than ever, and that he'd do it all again in a heartbeat.

Why? Because the choice to jump in is more important than the result. Obviously, decisions have consequences—but those consequences are what make the decisions meaningful in the first place.

So whether moving to Thailand, quitting your job, chasing your dream, going skydiving, doing weird new sex stuff, or proposing to your longtime partner, there's one thing I can absolutely guarantee you.

It sure as hell isn't boring.

No matter what the result is, you get excited. You perk up. You experience new things about yourself and the world that challenge everything you've ever believed, surprising you with new insights.

You feel fully alive.

Risks, losses, and the occasional setback are the price you pay to play the game. But if you're reading this book, and if you want to thrive, then you're here to play.

Let's introduce a totally unnecessary acronym none of us are going to remember: **F.I.—WTWTCH**

Fuck It—What's The Worst That Can Happen?

I've got good news. The worst-case scenario is to never do anything, to never take risks, and have your dream chucked on a pile of unpursued endeavors that is thousands of civilizations high. I think both of us can agree that literally anything is better than that.

You want to fear something? Learn to fear *that*.

The second-worst-case scenario is, you give your everything and it doesn't work out.

Who are you kidding, though? What it really is, is this: You give your everything and it doesn't work out *at first*.

Play the long game, and you're bound to succeed eventually. The setbacks along the way will teach you more than any book or guru ever could.

Believe that you'll make it there eventually, never quit, and you know what happens?

You *will* make it.

IT'S CLOSING TIME

Well my ENFP friend, we're getting close to the end of the book. Before I get to my emotional conclusion, I'd just like to thank, and congratulate, you for finishing this book.

Most people—like, almost everyone—buy books but never finish them. So if you're reading this it tells me you've got a bright future ahead of you.

I hope this book has served you well so far and can continue to be a resource you come back to. As one of my test readers told me, "It's awesome to have it with you. I take it out every time I feel down or lost or something and just have a quick read."

"YOU DON'T HAVE TO GO BACK"

Eda had just been reflecting on how hard it would be to return to Istanbul after her amazing experience in Europe. Eda had just quit her job and was finally living out her dream of traveling Europe alone for a month. As far as I could tell, she didn't have a plan afterwards and that was a good thing.

"To be clear, I'm not proposing we fall madly in love and you move to Prague. I mean your life before: You don't need to go back."

I told her about my own life, how I'd barely traveled before I moved to Costa Rica 11 years ago. How I had no interest in Europe before and moved here on a whim with a friend and yet here I was a decade on.

" I moved to Costa Rica with no money and a struggling freelance business. If anyone remotely responsible compared my income to the cost of living in Costa Rica, they would have strongly advised I stay home but I was naive and crazy and I did it."

People fall in love with cities like Prague and countries like Spain. Many of those people come to the same "F.I.—WTWTCH" conclusion.

Fuck It—What's The Worst That Can Happen?

You can see them teaching English, serving at bars, and managing hostels. You can also see them opening restaurants, owning hotels, and running some of the most profitable businesses in the city. Most of these "expat elite" moved here on a whim for cheap beer and pretty girls in the 90s or 2000s, but eventually, they grew up, spotted an opportunity, and applied the same fearlessness that helped them move here in the first place.

Remember the study on people with good vs bad luck? Life will always present us with opportunities. Some people will seize these opportunities while others will insist they need more of x, y, or z before they're able to make a change.

I can't help but laugh at Eda's journey so far and just how much it illustrates my belief: When you raise your hand and take the first risk, the universe starts to part oceans for you.

Eda, who I'm quite sure is an ENFP, took the first risk and quit her job. She then doubled down by taking her dream trip (instead of keeping it as a mental escape to get through the day). Two days into her dream trip, who does Eda, who wants to find a new income and move to Europe, match with on Bumble and spend her next three days with?

The world's #1 coach for ENFPs focused on life design, making big changes, working for yourself, and moving abroad.

I hope as Eda is reading this on her flight to Italy, she realizes how close she is to the new life she wants and that she has everything she needs to make it happen.

The other time

Some might read the above and say, "Sure but it isn't that easy for most people!"

Now I'm not going to point out that it used to be 3 Turkish Lira to $1 USD and is now 30. Or that Eda grew up in a conservative family. Or that she needed to fill out a crazy amount of forms to even get a visa to Europe.

On the other side are people who run from growth opportunities. In March, I was visiting The Netherlands for A State of Trance 1000 and I decided to organize a free meetup for YouTube subscribers and clients. It was a last-minute, relatively relaxed affair. Dinner and drinks with half a dozen interesting people.

"I am not able to meet up Tuesday (super busy after two months of procrastination; January and February always seem to be impossible months to do what I am supposed to do), but I wish you a great time in Amsterdam."

Just sit back and think about it. You have someone who is clearly in a cycle of struggle, the kind of cycle of struggle she knows I help my ENFP clients overcome. I am personally encouraging her to come out for a free evening to spend four or five hours with myself and other ENFPs who could likely help and encourage her.

And she is choosing to stay home to procrastinate on work she hasn't done in two months and most definitely did not do that night either.

"Luck" is only recognized as easy or obvious by others after someone has the courage to take a chance and then experiences the benefits. Then the armchair life critics like to say, "Well yes, I would have done the same thing *then*, but *my* situation is so different..."

WHAT'S NEXT?

While one acquaintance of mine is absolutely positive her people know what's up and she is very insistent on recruiting me to join them in the afterlife, I am still very confident in saying: No one knows what happens when we die.

And you will die.

It might be decades from now of very natural causes in the most peaceful of circumstances or it could, just maybe, be in a couple minutes when your smoothie is contaminated with peanut butter.

OK, well, I could die in a couple minutes. You likely have at least a few hours, if not days.

Damn you, peanut allergy!

And since you only have a few days, or perhaps 50 years, left to live, wouldn't it be a good time to ask the question, "what the hell for?"

While we don't know what will happen when we die, we do know the #1 regret people have right before they do:

" I wish I'd had the courage to live a life true to myself, not the life others expected of me."

Pursuing your calling won't always be easy. You might run into some trolls on the bridges you'll cross. You might find yourself ripe out of shillings, a little light on coin, facing some serious obstacles from time to time.

Yet I swear this to you, as I similarly swore it to the group of guys I convinced to party with me in Mexico the night before their 6 a.m. flight:

Many years from now, lying ill on your bed with death at the door, looking back on your life, I know you'll want to go back and trade it all—every moment from this day to that—just for one chance. One chance to come back and tell fear, doubt, and self-sabotage that it can try and take your time, chirp in your ear, disturb your sleep, but it will never take your freedom!

Whether it is your freedom to join me at the colosseum night club in Puerta Vallarta Mexico at 3 a.m. on a Tuesday night in 2005 or your freedom to CHOOSE to live your calling.

I may have paraphrased a bit of that speech from a movie. My memory is fuzzy. Perhaps it was Avatar?

My friend Monty used to always say, "Life's short, then you die," and truer words have never been spoken.

OK, that's a lie. He actually said, "Life's hard, then you die," but that quote didn't fit my message so I changed it.

You can choose whichever resonates with you most.

Whichever quote you've chosen, you now must decide how you spend that life of yours. One *radical idea* might be to do the thing you were put here to do. I can confidently say that because at the moment, I am writing. I would be less confident in making that challenge during the years of 2016-2021 when I didn't write anything.

So if you are also a writer, write. A painter? Paint. An entrepreneur? Make, create, and give value. A singer? Well, you already know this one. If you're a singer, you better open your mouth and belt out those words because the rest of us mother fuckers are waiting to dance.

The End
Dan "Not a Zombie Robot" Johnston

ABOUT DAN

Dan wrote this book. He also wrote this part about himself. Is it cool if he switches to first person now? Alright.

If you enjoyed this book and would like to connect with me more, here are the best ways to do it. Generally you can find me by looking up Dreams Around The World anywhere.

Email Newsletter — I mentioned this a few pages ago. You can subscribe to hear from me here:

YouTube — I have published over 400 videos on YouTube. I've recently grown tired of YouTube's algorithm and publish less frequently. Still, you can spend a month or two consuming my back catalogue. The majority of my videos were created for ENFPs.
www.YouTube.com/@ENFP

Podcast — Aside from my emails, this is the most likely place to consistently hear from me going forward.
www.DreamsAroundTheWorld.com/Podcast (or search for "Dreams Around The World" wherever you listen.)

Instagram — I prefer to live in the moment and I generally buy more plane tickets than I post pictures or stories. Still, you can follow me and DM me on IG. I'll reply within 1 - 30 days. @thedanjohnston

Email: I read every email I receive...eventually. Please don't send me your life story as one 37 sentence paragraph.
dan@dreamsaroundtheworld.com

Review Request

If you've enjoyed this book and want to support my writing, and support other ENFPs in discovering this book and becoming a force for positive change, the best thing you can do is leave a review wherever you bought this book...and if you're so inclined, on other sites selling the book as well.

This is the best way to spread the word and help others discover this book.

Thank you.

Questions?

From time to time I answer questions on my Podcast or YouTube channel on just about anything. If you've got a question related to this book you can submit it here. I'd love to hear from you.

www.DreamsAroundTheWorld.com/AskDan

READER RESOURCES

There is SO MUCH I wanted to include in this book. Some ended up in the appendix while other parts I feel are really valuable just didn't fit well in the book. So what I've done is create a series of resources for you. You can find the main resource page here:

www.DreamsAroundTheWorld.com/Calling

UPDATES

Are you one of those ENFPs who LOVES getting emails? Wow, what a coincidence because I was thinking of sending you a few emails.

Basically, I'll email you when:
- I create some kind of new bonus, extra, or training for readers of this book.
- I'm travelling and organizing a local reader meetup wherever I'm visiting.
- I am hosting any kind of live event, whether in person or online.
- I release a new book.
- I've been told some of my emails are absolute works of art. Others are pretty half assed.

You can get both the works of art and half assed emails here:

www.DreamsAroundTheWorld.com/ReaderList

ADDITIONAL RESOURCE
ENFP AUDIO PROGRAM

While writing the section of this book on fear and reprogramming your beliefs I had one of those inspired ENFP moments: What if I made an audio program for readers? Something they could listen to daily to help re-train their minds and instill useful beliefs?

So I went with it.

I've created a 7 part (7 day) audio series. The idea is to listen to one audio each day either first thing in the morning or before bed.

Or whenever. Really, if you listen every day you're doing pretty damn good and who am I to get all pedantic about your scheduling?

You can get access to the full audio series, at no cost, here: www.DreamsAroundTheWorld.com/CallingAudio

ADDITIONAL RESOURCE
ENFP ENTREPRENEUR TRAINING

Alright at this point I know you're like "Dude, if you mention ENFP Unleashed one more time I'm going to spite convert to being an ESTJ."

I totally get it, but I still need to give you access to that free 60 minute training from the program that shall not be named again. This is one of the 12 trainings members of the not to be named program have access to.

You can get access to the training here:
www.DreamsAroundTheWorld.com/CallingEntrepreneurs

ADDITIONAL RESOURCES
COOL ENFP TRAINING SERIES

I created a training series for ENFPs which is served up via email. You get a new email every day for a few weeks: Each one contains some kind of story, lesson, or insight. It's pretty entertaining and, dare I say, valuable. All the content is unique and different than what you've read in this book.

You can signup for the training series here:
www.DreamsAroundTheWorld.com/CallingENFP

GOING FURTHER

How I Support My Fellow ENFPs

Throughout this book you might hear me mention something I learned from a client or that happened at one of my events. To keep the confusion to a minimum, I'm going to share a brief nugget on each of the main ways I work with ENFPs.

ENFP Unleashed is a 12-week training which includes live coaching and a supportive community. It includes extras like the Superstar Series where I interview ENFPs who have achieved incredible things and get into detail about how they did it. As of this writing, I personally host group coaching sessions with members at least a few times a month.

One-on-One Coaching. My availability for one-on-one coaching varies tremendously by my writing and travel schedule, but you can always check my availability on the Work with Me page of my website.

In Person Events: I try to host one multi day in person event a year if time allows and enough people are interested.

The Free Freelancer is an intensive training program I run once per year for all NF types, although the members are mostly ENFPs. The program is for anyone who intends to build a successful freelancing, consulting, or coaching business and wants to learn business and marketing strategies specifically for NF types. I believe ENFPs want win-win relationships and care as much about giving value and having a positive impact as they do about making money and the lifestyle benefits of entrepreneurship.

For more details on all of the above and links to the specific pages, you can visit www.DreamsAroundTheWorld.com/Further

APPENDIX

ENFPS, RAPID CHANGE, AND AI

Avoid getting trapped in one lane. Trust me... it happens easier than you think. No offense, but I didn't set out in 2016 to become Mr. ENFP. Some videos went viral, I enjoyed working with ENFPs, and here we are.

Along the way I realized that we can play a huge role in making the world a better place, and I am happy I primarily work with ENFPs, but I'd be lying if I said momentum didn't play a big role. If I were deleted from the internet as well as your mind Men in Black style, would I jump right into working with ENFPs again? I have no idea.

Ditto on living in Prague. I am happy to live in Prague but damn, when I came here in 2014, I had plans for some serious global adventures in 2015... but the furnished apartments I saw sucked and I wanted a good bed, so I furnished a flat, met a girl, and here we are...

Intelligent people build on their past successes and use their momentum, but I would advise against too many anchors. Keep yourself minimalist, nimble, and open to starting something new.

In theory, there are few, if any, other personality types as suitable to adapt and change with the world as ENFPs. Perhaps the coming years may even be a "be careful what you wished for" situation for us. Whatever comes, know that you as an ENFP are equipped to understand, learn, and adapt as fast or faster than anyone else on the planet.

Also remember that wealth, income, and jobs are all relative. You might see a new headline like "Negative 3% growth!" And, okay, this does suck and some people will lose their jobs but as someone who has lived in countries with 10, 20, 30% unemployment, let me tell you that life still goes on.

ENFPs and AI

AI is as terrifying as it is exciting. While some praise the innovative potential, others are terrified of what we might unleash. In my opinion the proponents are often narcissists or super geeks who don't really like other humans.

We ENFPs speak a lot about change and our need for variety and excitement, so in theory you'd assume we'd be over the moon excited about innovations like AI.

Not exactly.

I love change within my own life within a system that is relatively easy to understand and predict. Knowing I can always go back to Canada and crash at any number of homes gives me the freedom to take more risks. But these things stack up in turbulent times. As society experiences large shifts, many people in our lives might as well. Suddenly, as an ENFP, we are change stacked upon change upon change upon change.

So if you, like myself, go to a dark place when you start watching YouTube videos on AI, know that you aren't alone.

Yet the more I think about AI, assuming we avoid a complete collapse of civilization, the more I am convinced ENFPs will thrive in the coming years.

Surprisingly to some, artificial intelligence and automation are killing white collar jobs much faster than blue collar jobs. There are no robots building homes or driving trucks yet, but there is software that's happy to do the low-level work of many lawyers, accountants, and other paper pushers.

It's also creeping into writing and design, two areas close to my heart, as I train many freelancers in my program The Free Freelancer. This got me thinking about the future of my past and future clients. Is there one?

I came back with a resounding yes. In The Free Freelancer, I have always taught my members to focus on being in the top 5% of their industry and to focus entirely on how they can give tremendous value while establishing themselves as experts.

This is how I went from charging $16 an hour as a freelance writer to $125+ within a year of starting out and while moving to Central America without losing any clients.

So yes, ChatGPT is going to take away A LOT of low-level writing jobs, but those were always shit jobs and they'd been outsourced to India and the Philippines for at least a decade.

This book, and my work in general, is about helping you find and pursue your calling, which always means being great at what you're doing. At least for now, AI isn't going to take that from you. In fact, it might just empower you to breeze past the boring work and become exponentially productive and focused only on what you do best.

To sum things up:
- AI will bring huge levels of change and similar levels of opportunities.
- Assuming we don't end up in The Matrix, there will be plenty of opportunities and entirely new industries created by AI.
- ENFPs are exceptional learners, adapters, and innovators who have the potential to thrive in the next iteration of our societies.

When it comes to thriving as an entrepreneur in the future, I will share the same advice I have given clients for years. The same advice that applied when competing with outsourced cheap labor or automations:
- Be One of The Best
- Be Trusted + Valued for Your Knowledge AND Opinions
- Embrace Your Personality and Be Excited for Change

Of course, even in the worst of times, those who are smart, adaptable, and hard-working always have options and can do well. There is plenty of argument for being happier and more satisfied when we focus on the basics, such as friends and family—the types of things people tend to focus on when times are a bit tougher and they aren't constantly on the grind.

While the above is all true, I must admit there is a part of me that is not overly optimistic about the future. If big tech is any indication, consolidated power and consolidated influence, like with Google or Facebook, is terrible for society and individuals. These companies have time and time again shown a complete disregard for individual happiness and instead prioritize spreadsheets and profits.

Nevertheless, I believe each of us MUST have an optimistic view of the future or else we are absolutely doomed. We can only be motivated to create a great life if we see a great future. I would much rather be happy while creating my great life and then suddenly get liquefied in a mushroom cloud than spend my years fearful of said mushroom cloud only to wake up at age 60 a broke loser in an otherwise utopian society.

ARE ENFPS WIRED FOR MONOGAMY?

"Since meeting you I don't believe any ENFP should ever
be monogamous. I never thought men were meant to be,
but now I don't think ENFP women are either."
—Anonymous INTJ

Yes, I understand the questionable nature of including a chapter on this topic when the initial version of this book was written while I was in a great six-year-long, monogamous relationship.

But hey, I'm not right now, and what could be more ENFP than questioning and adjusting your views as your circumstance change?

So let's jump right into things with a quote from a recent date I had.

" I was speaking to another ENFP friend about this too. Both of us have been radiant ever since we became single."

"Wow, you just gave me a lot to think about," I told my date, a fellow ENFP.

Since being single (for about a year at this stage), I've really been questioning traditional relationships. While in my relationship I felt happy and satisfied, my friends claimed single Dan was an entirely new person in terms of energy and zest.

Initially I figured this was more of a male thing. It's well understood that a "man in the wild" or in a new relationship will experience a boost in testosterone, which can lead to more energy and confidence, as well as a more vibrant outlook on life.

But here was an ENFP telling me her and her female ENFP friend had the same experience.

Of course, there could be many explanations for this. If someone is in a restrictive or just plain terrible relationship, of course they're going to bounce back with extra zest in their step.

This in no way means monogamy or long-term relationships are out of the question. It could just as easily mean you just need to find the right relationship.

But hey, I'd like to have some fun today, so I'm going to throw out a bold statement here and see if I can justify it:

For the majority of ENFPs, monogamy is less appealing and less beneficial than for most other people.

Yes, some people jump into a long-term, monogamous relationship because of true love. Absolutely.

But many of the "very pro-monogamy and long-term relationship" people I meet also express things to me like:

" I don't like dating. I hate meeting people."

Can you and I agree that if someone dislikes dating and dislikes meeting new people that sticking with one person may, just maybe, be much more appealing?

For many people one of the big appeals of monogamy is saving themselves from awkward dates and uncomfortable situations.

Personally, I LOVE dating. First dates are one of my favorite things to do.

So say, if I and an INFJ who hates first dates were to meet... which of us would be gaining more from settling into a monogamous relationship?

Which of us would be missing out on something they found a lot of enjoyment in?

I've also heard this one from a lot of (non ENFPs):

" I need to know someone for a long time to get really comfortable with them so I can open up and be sexual."

Of course, this varies from person to person and sexual intimacy is a very personal and deep discussion to have. But for the sake of argument, can we agree that generally ENFPs are more comfortable with strangers and can open up and put ourselves out there easier than most people?

If the topic of sex is taboo in your culture or religion, just think about how quickly we are able to open up and make friends. Also, I have no idea how you made it this far in this book but thank you for sticking with me.

Come on, we're the "it feels like I've known you for years" personality!

> So perhaps, just maybe, it could be possible for an ENFP to be really comfortable, trusting, and open with someone (the right someone, of course) they've only known for a few dates or even a few hours.

With topics like sex, romance, love, and intimacy, I hesitate to break things down to the economics of it...but I'm still going to.

Say you have two people who meet and feel an incredible connection.

Chica and Chico.

Chica is an extrovert with an adventurous soul and a thirst for life. Chico is reserved, disciplined, and hard working.

Chica is a romantic soul who loves meeting new people and has always had a very passionate sex life. Chico is one handsome dude but has never been good at "talking to the ladies" and is more concerned with building a stable life and successful career.

The two can't get enough of each other and soon come to the "where is this going" talk.

Being the 2020s, eventually the topic of monogamy comes up. Well, Chica brings it up. Chico just took it for granted they'd only be with each other.

At the moment of the discussion Chica is seeing a few people. No one she wants to spend her life with, but each of the men and women she's seeing bring something positive to her life. Chico occasionally meets girls from Tinder but generally just focuses on his friends and work.

So here's the question...

Is it an equal ask of both Chica and Chico to be monogamous? Is it fair? Are they both making the same sacrifice?

If you ask me, Chico is giving up very little. Chico is wired for monogamy and is thrusting his life plans and his belief system on Chica. Since monogamy is the publicly professed norm most everywhere in the world, he has plenty of arguments to play with and guilt to throw her way.

Of course she's wrong for wanting to be with more people, he might say.

But what is Chico really sacrificing?

On the other hand, Chica would be ending multiple positive relationships that have been adding to her life. She'd be losing a sense of freedom and adventure close to her heart.

Bad Monkey

I'm allergic to peanuts. If I eat peanuts I can die.

If I'm moving in with someone and we discuss "are peanuts allowed in the apartment?" the two outcomes of this discussion are not equal.

To remove peanuts from the home means they miss out on eating a food they enjoy.

To keep peanuts in the home means I might die.

It is not a coin toss discussion.

I do not think monogamy is a coin toss discussion. For some people, monogamy is a dream they've been wired to embrace since forever. A chance to escape awkward dates and loneliness alike.

For others, monogamy means losing aspects of freedom, adventure, romance, and love that may very well be a driving force in their being.

So are ENFPs wired for monogamy? **I have no idea.**

Well, that isn't true. There's no evidence humans were ever really monogamous until property rights, religion, and other external pressures began forcing the issue. See the book "Sex at Dawn" for more on this.

The question is, given our societal and family belief structures and the benefits of having a long-term partner in crime, should ENFPs be monogamous? Should you be monogamous?

That isn't a question I can answer here. The purpose of this is to get you thinking and questioning. And if you're one of the many ENFPs not satisfied in your relationship, you need to know that it isn't necessarily your fault. I also included it for all the ENFPs already in an alternative relationship or seriously thinking about one. Know that I've spoken to many of you one-on-one and you're not alone in this consideration. In fact, among atheist and agnostic ENFP women, it might be more common to desire, or at least ponder, a more open relationship than not.

If you're dating a more conservative person, it's not surprising if they make you feel like something is wrong with you.

"Why can't you settle down?"

"You're never happy"

But maybe you're not happy because you've been trying to force yourself into a broken model? Maybe you're not happy because you're trying to live against your nature.

If a shark stops swimming, they die. Perhaps there is nothing wrong with a desire to keep moving, keep experiencing new things, and, heaven forbid, to never settle or settle down.

I would love to deepen my knowledge of this topic. While I am doing my best asking around on ENFP Unleashed group coaching sessions, at my live events, in bars, and on dates, I'm only one man! So I set up an "ENFP Love Life" Survey here: www.DreamsAroundTheWorld.com/nakedenfps

Naturally, it is anonymous and only takes a few minutes to fill out.

A SPACE FOR YOUR THOUGHTS & NOTES